Enoch's
Blessing

A Modern English Paraphrase
of Enoch's Ancient Writings

by

Michael Fickess

"And for as long as I saw this,
I continually showered my affection
on the Lord of Glory…" *Enoch 36:4*

Table of Contents

Foreword

The book of Enoch could be one of the most important writings to understand as we approach the end of this age. The Lord said that the end of the age would be like "the time of Noah" and this book is about the times leading up to Noah.

The book of Enoch is quoted in canon Scripture as if it were Scripture. Some of the Lord's own teachings and parables seem to have been based on it, but it was not canonized in the Protestant Bible. Personally, I think that was the right call. Why?

The books that composed canon Scripture had to meet the highest standards of verification and authentication. For example, the entire New Testament can be verified by the writings of the Early Church Fathers (the direct disciples of the twelve disciples of the Lord), with the exception of just eleven verses, none of which was considered crucial for doctrine. Though there was no question that the book of Enoch was authentic, there were serious questions about some passages that seemed to have been interjected by another author/s, since the flow and spirit were so different from the rest of the book. This left too many questions about the corruption of the only manuscripts in their possession. Every time I have read this book, I too have felt there were some passages that do not seem to have been written by the same author.

Believing there is merit to the reasoning of the canonizing council, I do not think this book should be read as canon Scripture. But that does not mean that it does not have merit. None of the Christian books written since the first century are canon Scripture either, but they can have merit. The book of Enoch may have more merit and important understanding than any other non-canonized writing because parts of it were quoted in the books that are now canon Scripture. Also, it is written about the times that the Lord said the end of this age would be like. Even so, I recommend this only for mature believers.

To many people, anything they are not familiar with is weird. Let's face it, the spiritual realm is weird to everyone and incomprehensible to the natural mind. However, we also need to understand that there is good weird and bad weird. There are weird beings in the spiritual realm as we see throughout Scripture: the Seraphim, Cherubim, those that appeared as wheels with many eyes to Ezekiel, etc. Almost all of them are good.

Anyone who is closed to anything they are not familiar with has become what the Lord called an "old wineskin," too rigid and inflexible to receive the new. The book of Enoch will challenge your understanding, but we should be careful not to throw things out that we may not understand, unless it is in conflict with Scripture. If our understanding cannot be stretched, then we are the rigid old wineskins.

We must keep an open mind to continue to mature in the Lord, but having an open mind does not mean that we accept everything. We are exhorted to "try all things," test them, and hold fast to the good. If we are going to understand the spiritual realm and be at home in it as every "new creation" person should be, then we must learn that because something is strange to us, it is not necessarily bad.

In this rendering of the book of Enoch, Michael Fickess has done a remarkable job. He not only gives a lot of explanation to the weird, but also brings a practical and timely application to the message it has for today. I highly recommend reading his footnotes as you go.

— Rick Joyner, Founder and Executive Director of
MorningStar Ministries

Introduction
Encountering Enoch

Our first encounter with Enoch in the Bible is shrouded in mystery. The Book of Genesis simply states: **"Enoch walked faithfully with God; then he was no more, because God took him away" (Genesis 5:24).** This is one of the shortest biographies ever written and it leaves a lot of unanswered questions about Enoch's life. From this short passage, we have no idea what he accomplished or how he walked with God so closely in an era that was overrun with wickedness and godlessness.

Enoch is also mentioned in Hebrews chapter 11 among the giants of faith. Here, Paul gives an even more mysterious explanation: **"By faith Enoch was taken from this life, so that he did not experience death" (Hebrews 11:5).** Elijah is the only other prophet who we know was taken to heaven without experiencing death. However, Scripture gives us all of the details of Elijah's chariot ride and very few clues concerning the life of Enoch.

Historical Context of the Book of Enoch

The book of Enoch is not canonized Scripture, but it is given credibility by canonized Scripture. The Apostle Jude quoted directly from the book of Enoch in his epistle (see

Jude 1:14-15). This demonstrates that the early church fathers were not only familiar with the book of Enoch, but they also accepted it as a legitimate source of spiritual authority. My purpose in providing this paraphrase is not to suggest that we should add the book of Enoch to the Bible. However, the book of Enoch makes an excellent companion for our ongoing study of the Bible because it sheds light on what other prophets saw in both the Old and New Testaments. Its value is not in introducing new doctrine, but in seeing eternal truths with fresh clarity. If you're reading this book the way I hope you will, then the revelations in it will propel you back into searching the Scriptures with renewed excitement.

As I read the book of Enoch and worked on this paraphrase, I was struck by how many of Enoch's descriptions reflect what Jesus Christ spoke. For example, I never understood what Jesus meant when He said, **"When an impure spirit comes out of a person, it goes through arid places seeking rest and does not find it" (see Matthew 12:43).** Enoch actually describes these arid places in great detail.

Likewise, when Jesus referred to the **"days of Noah"** in Matthew 24, He was speaking to an audience that was well acquainted with the book of Enoch, which may have given them more understanding of what He was referring to. It is important to understand the worldview of the Jews, the ones who Jesus preached and ministered to, as well as Christ's own worldview. In the time of Christ, the Torah and the prophets were the primary authorities, but other books that were handed down, such as the book of Enoch, were also rigorously studied and were very influential in the way Jews understood and engaged with God, angels, and demons.

To help the reader receive everything intended from this book, I have included many references to Scriptures and detailed notes to illuminate the many connections between this book and canon Scripture. There's a chance that as you read, you'll be shocked by how well the book of Enoch aligns with the Bible.

Also as you read, you may notice that much of what you will see and hear happening in this text is remarkably similar to what you might experience in Daniel, Ezekiel, or Revelation. Likewise, many of the prophetic declarations made here are similar to declarations made in Scripture. However, I encourage you to be like the Bereans, who **"examined the Scriptures every day, to see if what Paul said was true" (see Acts 17:11).** There may be cases where the book of Enoch expands your understanding of some of the Scriptures that you've read before, but never fully grasped.

The Hebrew Mindset

King Solomon explained, **"It is the glory of God to conceal a matter; to search out a matter is the glory of kings" (see Proverbs 25:2).** The reason that God gives us mysteries in the Bible is so that we will be changed through the process of "searching them out." Our act of seeking is meant to involve the whole man, so that the whole man will be transformed in the process.

Unfortunately, in mainstream Western Christianity, searching the Scriptures has often remained a purely rational approach that relies upon a Greek system of analysis and logic. The underlying mindset of this Greek approach is that we think we can learn everything there is to know about God through mere rational engagement with the Scriptures. This is an incredibly destructive mindset because it has often reduced the Christian faith to a narrow set of doctrines, precepts, and practices, resulting in a weak and anemic body of believers. The fruit of this mindset is usually boredom, apathy, and hearts that have grown cold towards our first love.

Fortunately, both the Bible and church history demonstrate that when the Holy Spirit comes in power, He awakens every part of our being. As a result, the whole man is able to participate in **"all the powers of the age to come" (see Hebrews 6:5).** There is a vast difference between knowing all of the Scriptures about angels and actually talking with one. Likewise, there is a vast difference between knowing all of the facts and doctrines about Jesus and actually encountering the living Christ in a real and tangible way. The former will have you confident in your great knowledge, and you might even be able to teach others what you know. But the latter will leave you weeping on the floor and forever changed.

In stark contrast to the Greek approach, the Hebrew mindset embraces both rigorous study of the Scriptures and direct experience and encounters with the Presence of God. This is why Jesus told the teachers of the law, **"you are in error because you do not know the Scriptures or the power of**

God" (see Matthew 22:29). He was calling them back to their true heritage and giving His definition of true "balance."

In the Hebrew mindset, the mysteries of God are engaged with the underlying mindset that God is infinitely greater than we can fathom and that **"His thoughts are higher than our thoughts and His ways are higher than our ways" (see Isaiah 55:9).** This mindset acknowledges that His plans for us are greater than anything we could possibly comprehend. As believers under the New Covenant, we can actually begin to engage tangibly with the Holy Spirit, with angels, and with the Spirit realm.

Another central aspect of Hebrew thinking is that it is circular. What was lost in the beginning is restored in the end. When we lay down our lives, we get new ones. The book of Enoch fits into this circular pattern because the first prophet used this book to bless the last prophetic generation.[1]

The "Thin Gold Line"

There is a thin gold line that runs through all of church history, traversed by countless mystics, prophets, revivalists, and ordinary saints whose lives were devoted to prayer. These are the ones who engaged the Scriptures with the whole man. Their hearts, their spirits, their minds, and even their mortal bodies were often flooded with the ecstasy that comes from

---

1 In Genesis 20:7, Abraham is the first man in the Bible who is directly referred to as a "prophet." However, Jude makes it clear that Enoch "prophesied" long before Abraham (see Jude 1:14).

encountering the glory of the risen Christ. They fasted and prayed and crucified their carnal nature because they wanted to see the promises of God not merely taught, but truly made manifest in all the earth. The church owes nearly all of its advances throughout the centuries to this thin gold line.

The book of Enoch was written for those who would like to travel the thin gold line today. As the first prophet and mystic, Enoch walked with God. He tapped into the power of the new creation that was released through Christ, who is **"the Lamb slain before the foundation of the world" (see Revelation 13:8).** He boldly reclaimed the relationship with God that Adam had forfeited, even thousands of years before Christ walked among us. This was not because of his own righteousness, but from his encounter with the only One who has the power to redeem us from sin and death—the eternal living Christ.

Many people have attempted to use the book of Enoch to support all manner of speculation and conspiracy about what may have happened on the earth before the flood. I am not denying that there may be some merit to some of these theories, but a focus on these side issues ignores the central purpose of the book. The book of Enoch clearly states that its purpose is to bless the righteous, and I am convinced that the primary blessing it offers is revelatory insight into how to walk with God in a more tangible way.

Enoch's Engagement with the "Spirit Realm"

In both the Old and New Testament Scriptures, we see many strange and supernatural things happening: Axe heads float, superhuman giants are overcome, the Red Sea is parted, sundials go backward, and the list could continue for many pages. We also see some descriptions of the "Spirit realm" and spiritual beings that go far beyond our rational ability to grasp: the four living creatures described by Ezekiel and John are probably the best example of this. The book of Enoch is no less strange than the Bible stories we all learned in Sunday school.

Much of the book of Enoch describes revelatory journeys to places in what many refer to as the "Spirit realm." For instance, heaven, the abyss, Sheol (the Jewish term for hell under the Old Covenant), and the places where fallen angels will be imprisoned are included. A careful study of the Scriptures shows that these places are not only found in the Bible, but are a higher and more permanent dimension of reality than the world we presently live in. This is why Jesus said, **"Heaven and earth will pass away, but My words will never pass away"** (see Matthew 24:35).

One of the truths that God is restoring to the church in this hour is the reality that we are meant to be **"seated with Christ in heavenly places"** (see Ephesians 2:6) in the here and now. God is in the process of expanding the thin gold line today; He is calling ordinary saints to become lost in the glory of encountering the living Christ. He is calling us to **"eagerly desire"** (see I Corinthians 14:1) prophetic experiences. He is calling us to continue maturing spiritually until we are living a prophetic lifestyle in which we are left utterly undone and transformed on a daily basis. We are moving from simply being impressed when there are a few periodic prophetic utterances happening in our meetings to truly walking by the Spirit and living in "two realms" continuously. This is what Paul called the "high calling" of God: it is the path that Enoch chose and it is the only path that will allow our generation to reach its true destiny (see Hebrews 12).

The idea of living this way might sound outlandish, but Jesus Himself compared those who are **"born of the Spirit"** with the wind, explaining that the wind **"blows wherever it pleases"** and **"you cannot tell where it comes from or where it is going" (see John 3:8).** He didn't say that the Holy Spirit would be blowing like the wind and going wherever He pleases: He said that we would be. Likewise, Paul explains that, **"Those who are led by the Spirit are sons of God" (see Romans 8:14).** The **"sons of God"** who are about to come on the global scene will be just as Jesus described, for God is restoring son-ship to the body of Christ, and we are beginning to walk in our full inheritance as children of God.

Based on the simple description that Jesus gave us in John chapter three, Enoch was tapping into the power of the New Covenant during the first chapter of earth's history. The reality of being born of the Spirit and being led by Him were made manifest in his life to the point that God was so pleased with him that He gave him a personal rapture. How, you ask, could he tap into the redemption of Christ long before the Lord of Glory walked this earth? The clues are in the text itself, where

Enoch describes the living Christ in detail that is remarkably similar to John's description in Revelation chapter one. Our God lives outside of this limited domain of time and space where we now dwell, and the blood of the Lamb was sprinkled once and forever above this limited earthly domain, so that all of creation might be redeemed once and for all, from the beginning to the end of it (see Colossians 1:15-20). Enoch was included in the **"one new man" (see Ephesians 2:15)** by faith, because this promise of total redemption is available to everyone who is "in Christ."

A careful reading of this book demonstrates that Enoch foresaw both the Old and New Covenants. For example, he saw many different features of the Holy Land before it was inhabited and noted that it was already a blessed place. He smelled the fragrant trees that would be used to produce the consecrated oil and incense of the priesthood. He saw the canopy of God's glory spread out over Sinai. He encountered the Living Christ in all of His power and glory. And he saw the New Jerusalem in all of its beauty and brilliance. Some have suggested that this exposes the book of Enoch as a fraud because he couldn't possibly have known these things would come. However, the same arguments have been made for the remarkable prophetic accuracy of the Book of Daniel. Rather than viewing this alignment and level of detail as a disqualifying feature, I see all of these things as exciting confirmations of the book of Enoch's authenticity.

The precise manner in which he saw these things is difficult to describe. However, we must remember that we serve an eternal, omniscient, and omnipresent God who is not limited by the domains of time and space that He has created. If we actually believe these eternal truths about the nature of God, then the reality that Enoch was able to transcend time and space in order to see these things by the Spirit actually makes good sense. This is the same kind of experience that John had in the Book of Revelation.

Many of those who have travelled the thin gold line have actually had similar experiences. If we are truly "seated with Christ in heavenly places," then our spirits are communing with an omnipotent, omnipresent, and omniscient God who also allows us to push past the limitations of this earthly realm to gain eternal spiritual insight and revelation. Rather than being a strange and mystical truth, this is actually meant to be a foundation of the Christian life. Paul explains that, as believers, we have full access to behold the living Christ with **"unveiled faces,"** so that we will be **"transformed into his likeness with ever-increasing glory" (see II Corinthians 3:18).** For those who want to dive deeper into the greater glory available to us under the New Covenant, I recommend the sequel to this book, *Paths of Ever-Increasing Glory: What Enoch's Ancient Writings Reveal About Christ's Supremacy and our Prophetic Destiny.* Using the scriptures as a firm foundation and the Book of Enoch for further illumination, this book explores topics such as the supremacy of Christ, angelic ministry, the cloud of witnesses, keys to walking with God as Enoch did, and much more.

It is true that "many antichrists have gone out into the world": demon spirits and fallen angels have deceived many through occult practices, witchcraft, spiritualism, eastern religions, and dangerous perversions of Christianity itself. However, it is only by fully engaging the Spirit of Christ that we will become empowered with heavenly glory, authority, and power to overcome the dark spirits that have deceived this world. In fact, they are the "giants in the land" that we are meant to displace with our authority as sons of God who are co-seated with Christ.

Restoring Awe and Wonder

A central feature of the book of Enoch is his continual awe of God and all that He has made. The things that he sees in the spirit realm are so monumental that he struggles to find the right language to express the immensity of God's glory that he is beholding. This book is a blessing for this generation because we need to reclaim our awe and wonder of God. I am convinced that one of the ways God will restore awe and wonder is by revealing Himself to us in greater ways. This is what Enoch describes as "[God] coming out of His canopy." If Enoch's words are truly inspired, then God is about to reveal Himself to us in a way that has never before been seen on the earth. This is why Joel prophesied the Holy Spirit would be poured out on all flesh, so that an entire generation would prophesy and see God's glory together (see Joel chapter 2).

It is time to begin hungering and thirsting for God and asking Him to fulfill His purpose for this generation. For too long our devotion to God has been held back by either striving or distraction. But what would happen if we laid aside our cell phones for a day and began walking the thin gold line? What would happen if we turned off the television and stopped to observe how the wind rustles the leaves in the trees? The amazing thing about Enoch is that he showed as much appreciation for God's dominion over the earth as he did for God's dominion over heaven. He was undone by his vision of heaven, but also noticed how God was continually speaking through the stars, the trees, and the rivers.

I am not suggesting that every Christian is going to directly experience what Enoch did in this life. However, I firmly believe that this is available for anyone who is hungry enough to lay hold of it. Many prophets and mystics have already traveled the thin gold line along with him, encountering the living Spirit of Christ and catching glimpses of the heavenly realms, and they are among the cloud of witnesses calling us to go deeper into the realm of the Spirit.

You will receive as much of God's Spirit as you hunger for. This is why I suggest reading this book with a contemplative mindset, while also reserving the right to analyze what you're reading. There's nothing wrong with stopping to examine and compare against the Scriptures to verify what you're reading, or even reject it. There's also nothing wrong with feeling a sense of awe and wonder as you encounter what Enoch saw through his writing. The value of all of these descriptions is that they expand our understanding and our appreciation of God's glory. My hope is that this book will trigger greater hunger for God in your life. The bread of His Presence is real, tangible, and fully available to you.

Why Enoch Matters Today

Enoch matters first and foremost because God says he does. He says it clearly in the Scriptures, where he is the first prophet recorded in the Book of Genesis and is again honored in Hebrews 11 among the giants of the faith. In addition to Enoch's endorsement by the testimony of Scripture, I have noticed that the Holy Spirit is using Enoch to minister to the body of Christ with increasing frequency. For example, mature apostles and prophets are reporting prophetic encounters with Enoch on a regular basis, and pastors and teachers are preaching about his life from the pulpit. As a result, believers are growing more interested in what we can learn from his life.

I believe that the book of Enoch was preserved, and yet hidden, until this hour because it has a critical message for our generation. In the first chapter, Enoch explains that the book is a blessing for "the elect and righteous, who will be living in the day of tribulation." It further explains that it is written "not for my [Enoch's] generation, but for a generation far in the future" (see Enoch 1:1-2). These verses outline the true purpose of the book: to minister to believers at the end of the age.

The book of Enoch has never been widely distributed and digested within the body of Christ because we weren't ready for it until now. It presents a view of the Spirit realm that is best understood by mature believers who are able to actually function in that realm through the Holy Spirit's power.

About this Paraphrase Version

The manuscript of the book of Enoch that we draw from today was kept alive by the Ethiopian Orthodox Church and the Eritrean Orthodox Tewahedo Church, both of whom have always regarded it as authentic, credible, and inspired by God. However, the ancient manuscripts they received were written long before the time of Christ. For example, the fragments of the book of Enoch that were found in the Dead Sea scrolls in Qumran in the West Bank can be dated to about 400 years before Christ. The version that is presented in this book is a modern paraphrase that I have written based on the 1917 English translation by R.H. Charles.

For the layperson, it may be important to clarify some terminology here: a translation actually goes back to the earliest manuscripts to decode the ancient languages in which a sacred text was written. The King James Version and New International Version are examples of Bible translations. A paraphrase uses a translation whose credibility is already established to re-word the sacred text so that it is more understandable. The Living Bible and The Message are examples of paraphrase Bibles.

The most recent reliable English translation of the book of Enoch that I've found was completed by R.H. Charles over 100 years ago. He was rigorous, thorough, and careful in his translation of the source texts. However, the simple age of this translation rendered it useless to most modern English speaking readers. The language is archaic, Shakespearean, and difficult to understand. As a result, most believers who took the trouble to find this forgotten book tended to put it back on the shelf because the R.H. Charles version is college-level reading, based on its vocabulary and sentence construction. (It includes countless phrases such as "mutual imprecations" that take some dictionary work to decode.) While I considered this project to be primarily a spiritual exercise, I brought with it the same academic rigor and integrity that I applied to my Master's degree in Middle Eastern history.

As I worked deep into the night on writing this paraphrase version, I was driven by two things: passion and the fear of the Lord. I wrote this because I passionately believe this book must be restored to the body of Christ in this hour. However, as I wrote each line, I also searched with a trembling hand for words that would reflect the text with both accuracy and clarity. I also added line breaks to give the book a more contemplative quality. In a few places, I have added words or verse numbers to give the reader greater clarity: in each case, I have used brackets [ ] so that the reader can clearly see which sections were enhanced.

As I wrote, my desire was to honor the thin gold line that has gone before me by honoring a text that many have considered inspired—myself included. And more than that, I want to give due honor to the man who God has honored in His Word. Because this is a paraphrase and not a translation, I chose to re-title it out of intellectual integrity. The book is named Enoch's Blessing because blessing our generation is the self-stated purpose of the Book of Enoch. Also, if any verses here are later found worthy of quoting, then this provides a distinguishing title from other translations that have already been written or which may be written in the future.

I felt very strongly that this book should be composed entirely of the works that are credited to Enoch, without any disruption from the books and fragments that are attributed to other authors. In Enoch's Blessing, I have included most of the writings which I consider to be authentic, inspired, and authored by Enoch: The Book of Enoch, Enoch's Journeys through Earth and Sheol, and The Parables. I did not include other ancient books that R.H. Charles included in his translation and I did not include Enoch 2 or Enoch 3 because most of these books are clearly from different authors.

The editorial choices that I've made allow this book to be more focused on the specific message that Enoch was given and allow this version to be composed entirely of Enoch's words. Hopefully, you'll agree that his message deserves our undivided attention. The chapter and verse divisions used by R.H. Charles are retained for easy comparison with other translations. The books included in this work can be heavily supported and cross-referenced with both Old Testament and New Testament Scriptures and are full of powerful insights that illumine the Word.

Up until this point, the book of Enoch has been surrounded by great controversy, but much of this is because the books were never properly separated, as I have attempted to do. The same academic arguments that attempted to discredit various books of canon Scripture have been used to try to discredit the writings that are included in this book. However, the fact that the apostles referenced these writings gives them a mark of credibility that is worthy of consideration. I believe God's hand was in the controversies that have surrounded Enoch's writings. The church was not ready to digest his writings until this hour, so it was right for the Holy Spirit to allow these controversies to continue for as long as He determined it should remain hidden.

I welcome your suggestions to improve the text or any critiques of the text itself. I am under no delusion that this text is perfect; however, I took great joy in the presence of the Lord that was with me as I wrote this. I hope that as you read Enoch's Blessing, you will experience the same awe and wonder of God that I felt as I was writing it.

The Book
Of Enoch

CHAPTERS 1-16

A Blessing for Future Generations

1 (1) These are the words of Enoch's blessing,
in which he blessed the righteous
and the chosen ones,
who will live in the time of tribulation,
when all the wicked
and those who have rejected God
will be removed.[2]

(2) And he began his prophecy, saying:

Enoch was a righteous man,
his eyes were opened by God,
and he saw this vision of
the Holy One in the heavens.

The angels revealed it to me,
and I heard everything from them,
and they gave me clarity as I saw these things,
which were not for my own generation,
but for a generation far in the future.[3]

---

2 Revelation 7 describes a distinct group of chosen ones, the 144,000 who bear the seal of God, in addition to a "great multitude" who will come out of the "great tribulation." One interpretation of this first chapter is that Enoch saw this last generation prophetically and wrote this book as a blessing to them.

3 This verse indicates that this book was written for those living at the end of the age. Similarly, Daniel's book was "sealed up until the time of the end" (see Daniel 12:4).

(3) Then he spoke about the elect
and prophesied about them:

The Great and Holy One
will come out from His canopy,[4]
(4) and the eternal God
will walk upon the earth.[5]

And on Mount Sinai
He will emerge from His tent
and make Himself known
with awesome strength
from the highest heaven.

(5) And everyone will be terrified,
and the Watchers will be shaken,[6]
and great fear and trembling
will overtake them in every place on earth.

(6) The high mountains will shake,
and the high hills will be flattened,

---

4 Compare to Psalm 18, in which the "brightness of [the Lord's] Presence" breaks forth from the "dark canopy" around Him (see Psalm 18:11-12).

5 This likely refers to Jesus Christ, who "became flesh and made his dwelling among us" (see John 1:14). He is the "eternal God" who also "walked the earth."

6 Watcher is a term that Enoch frequently uses to refer to fallen angels. The term "Watchers" signifies both their original high calling to watch over humanity, and their role in occult practices. The Bible also refers to a holy (or unfallen) "watcher" angel in Daniel 4:13-23 NKJV.

they will melt like wax before a flame,[7]
(7) and the earth will be completely split apart,[8]
and everyone on the earth will die,
and all mankind will be judged.

(8) But He will establish peace
through the righteous.[9]
He will protect [His] chosen ones
and put them under His mercy.[10]
They will all belong to God,[11]
and they will prosper,
and He will bless them.
He will help every one of them,
and light will come to them,
and He will establish peace through them.[12]

(9) See! The Lord is coming
with thousands upon thousands
of His holy ones to judge everyone,
and to convict all the ungodly

---

7 See Micah 1:4

8 See Zechariah 14:4

9 See Isaiah 9:7

10 This speaks of the New Covenant, in which we are positioned under the mercy that comes through Christ's shed blood (see I Peter 2:9-11).

11 See Isaiah 44:5

12 Note that this introductory chapter provides a list of nine specific blessings that Enoch declares over the final generation.

of all the corrupt things
that were done in their depravity,
and of all the harsh words
that godless sinners have spoken against Him.[13]

The Beauty and Order of Creation

2 (1) Watch everything that happens in heaven,
and notice how each orbit is established.
And look at the stars in the galaxies,
how they all rise and set in harmony
each one in the right season,
because they never leave their fixed locations.[14]

(2) Then look at the earth,
and notice what happens there from first to last,
how unwavering these things are,
and how none of these natural processes change,
so that you'll be able to comprehend God's works.

(3) Consider the summer and the winter,
how the whole earth is filled with water,
and clouds and dew and rain rest upon it.

---

13 This verse is quoted directly by Jude, an apostle of Christ, in Jude 1:14. This demonstrates that the book of Enoch was a trusted source of wisdom and spiritual insight among the early church fathers.

14 See Psalm 19:1.

3 (1) Consider how in the winter
all the trees look like they have withered
because they have shed all of their leaves,[15]
with the exception of fourteen trees,
which do not lose their foliage
but keep their old leaves
for two to three years
until the new growth comes.[16]

4 (1) Also, notice how in the days of summer,
the sun moves to a higher position
above the earth.
Then, you look for shade and shelter
because you feel the heat of the sun,
and the earth emanates with great heat,
so that you cannot even walk
on the soil or on the rocks
because they have become too hot.

5 (1) Consider how the trees cover themselves
with green leaves and bear fruit,
and now you can come to the full realization
of how God speaks through all of His creation,

---

15 It's notable that the first section after the introduction directs our attention back to the intricate order of creation, a contemplative stance that is often neglected in our fast-paced modern world.

16 Notice that Enoch has an interest in scientific classification: science can be in harmony with the things of God.

and you can recognize how He who lives forever
has made everything for a specific purpose.

(2) Everything that He has created
operates the same way from one year to the next
and on into eternity,[17]
He is their true purpose,[18]
and these functions never change,
but [everything in creation]
continues to fulfill its purpose.

(3) Consider how the sea and the rivers
fulfill their purpose and never change their tasks
outside of His appointed order.[19]

(4) In contrast, you have not been faithful,
because you have not done
what the Lord told you to do.
You have turned away from Him
and spoken proud and bitter words
speaking with impure mouths

---

17 Compare this chapter with Ecclesiastes 1:1-10.

18 Colossians 1:15-16 explains that everything was created through Christ and for Christ, who is the "firstborn of all creation." He is the purpose for all of creation: everything was made to glorify Him and reflect His perfect and divine nature.

19 Enoch's description of nature's consistency reflects the unchanging and perfect nature of God Himself (see Hebrews 13:8).

against God's greatness.
Oh, you hard-hearted people will not find peace.

(5) Therefore, you will despise your days,
and the years of your life will waste away,
and the years of your destruction
will be multiplied into eternal damnation,
and you will find no mercy.

(6a)[20] In those days, you will make your names
an eternal abomination to all of the righteous,
(6b) And everyone who curses will curse by you,
and you will be damned by
all of the sinners and godless,
(6c) And for you godless people,
there will only be a curse.[21]

(6d) But all the righteous will be filled with joy,[22]
(6e) And there will be forgiveness of sins,
(6f) And a manifestation of every kind
of mercy and peace and patience.[23]

---

20 The additional nomenclature of (6a), (6b), (6c), etc. is included so that this
text will be consistent with the R.H. Charles translation, from which it was
paraphrased.

21 Compare the curses listed in this chapter with those listed in Deuteronomy
27:14-26. Those who reject Christ and live godless lives remain under the curse of
sin and death.

22 See Romans 14:17.

23 See Galatians 5:22-23.

(6g) Salvation will come to them
as an exceedingly brilliant light.[24]
(6i) But for all of you sinners
there will be no salvation,
(6j) because a curse is resting on you.[25]

(7a) But for the chosen ones
there will be light and joy and peace,
(7b) and they will receive
the whole earth as an inheritance.[26]
(8) And then the elect will be
endowed with great wisdom,
and they will all be filled with life[27]
and [they will] never sin again,
either through ungodliness or pride:
everyone who is wise will walk humbly.

(9) And they will never again disobey Him,
they will never again sin
for all the days of their lives,
they will not experience death

---

24 See Isaiah 9:2 and Matthew 4:15-18.

25 This seems to imply that there is no forgiveness for anyone. However, a careful reading demonstrates that for some "there is forgiveness of sins" and "salvation comes as a great light," but for others the "curse" of sin and death remains. This is the case because man has been given the freedom either to accept or reject Christ's redemption.

26 See Psalm 2:8, Matthew 5:5.

27 See John 10:10.

by God's anger or wrath,
but they will complete the [appointed] number
of the days of their life.
And the peace in their lives
will continually increase,
And their joyful years will be multiplied,
until they find eternal gladness and peace,
all the days of their life.[28]

Fallen Angels Corrupt Mankind

6 1) After the children of men were multiplied,
beautiful and graceful daughters
were born to them.[29]
(2) And the angels, the children of heaven,
saw them and lusted after them, and said to each other:
'Come, let us choose wives
from among the children of men
and conceive children for ourselves.'

(3) And Semjaza,[30] their leader, said to them:

'I am afraid that you will not actually do
what you have promised, and that I alone

---

28 Note that this chapter also includes a list of blessings declared by Enoch, which is the self-stated purpose of this first section.

29 See Genesis 6:1-4 for a biblical parallel to this chapter.

30 Semjaza means "infamous rebellion."

will pay the penalty of this great sin.' [31]

(4) And they answered him as one and said:

'Let us all swear an oath,
and all bind ourselves as one
by swearing together
that we will not abandon this plan
but will do this together.'

(5) Then they all swore an oath together
and bound themselves by mutual curses to do it.
(6) There were two hundred of them;
they descended in the days of Jared[32]
to the summit of Mount Hermon,
and they called it Mount Hermon,
because they had sworn and bound themselves
by shared oaths that were sworn upon it.[33]

(7) And these are the names of their leaders:

---

31 Enoch provides names for angels throughout the book. Some are also in the Scriptures, while others are not. However, the basic principle that angels have names is biblical. Also, the names of the archangels that Enoch provides later in the text are substantiated by Jewish tradition and rabbinical writings.

32 See Jared's genealogy in Genesis chapter 5.

33 Mount Hermon was also the place where Og, King of Bashan, ruled until the Israelites defeated him (see Joshua 12:5). It also featured in Psalm 133. Many scholars also consider it to be the site of Christ's transfiguration.

Semiazaz, their leader, Arakiba, Rameel, Kokabiel, Tabiel, Ramiel, Danel, Ezeqeel, Baraqijal, Asael, Armaros, Batarel, Ananel, Zaqiel, Samsapeel, Satarel, Turel, Jomjael, and Sariel.

(8) These are their captains of tens.

7 (1) And all of them took wives, and each chose one for himself, and they became intimate with them and defiled themselves, and they taught them about magic and witchcraft, and the cutting of roots, and made them acquainted with plants.[34]

(2) And they became pregnant, and bore great giants, whose height was three thousand ells: [35]

(3) They consumed everything that men had acquired. And when humanity could no longer sustain them, (4) the giants turned against them and began to devour mankind.

---

34 The "cutting of roots" and "acquaintance with plants" here probably refers to the use of roots and plants in magic, sorcery, or witchcraft rather than for purposes of growing food or medicine.

35 Like the cubit, an ell is an ancient measurement. Using comparisons to other units of ancient times, some scholars speculate these giants would have stood about 450 feet tall. However, this estimate may be wrong because we do not know the exact length of the ell used in pre-flood civilizations.

(5) And they began to sin against birds, and beasts,
and reptiles, and fish, and to eat each other's flesh,
and drink each other's blood.[36]

(6) Then the earth cried out in accusation
against these lawless ones.

8 (1) And Azazel taught men to make swords, knives,
shields, and breastplates.
He taught them about the metals of the earth
and metalsmithing,
how to make bracelets and ornaments,
the use of antimony,
the beautifying of the eyelids,
all kinds of precious stones,
and all coloring pigments.[37]

(2) And as their godlessness increased,
their sexual sin and deception increased,
and they became completely corrupted in every way.

Semjaza taught spell-casting and root-cuttings,
Armaros the undoing of spells,
Baraqijal taught astrology,

---

36 This chapter is often used to speculate that fallen angels were involved in
genetic engineering. Some consider this to be mere speculation, while others draw
parallels with modern genetic engineering and its potential problems.

37 Antimony is an element in our Periodic Table of Elements that was often used
in making cosmetics in ancient times. It can also be used to create different alloys.

Kokabel the constellations,
Ezeqeel the knowledge of the clouds,
Araqiel the signs of the earth,
Shamsiel the signs of the sun,
and Sariel the course of the moon.[38]

And as more men died, they cried out,
and their cry rose up to heaven.

The Archangels Respond

9(1) And then Michael, Uriel, Raphael,
and Gabriel looked down from heaven
and saw all of the blood that was being shed
on the earth, and all of the wickedness
that was happening.

(2) And they said to each other:

'The earth itself is now crying out
and reverberating with the sound
of man's intense suffering
to the point that it has reached
the very gates of heaven.' [39]

---

38 The central lesson of this chapter is that astrology, witchcraft, and sorcery
are rooted in the kingdom of darkness. The heavens and the earth were made to
declare God's glory, but the fallen angels sought to pervert everything from its true
purpose.

39 See Genesis 6:5 and Genesis 6:11.

3) Now the souls of men appealed
to the angels of heaven and said,

"Bring our cause before the Most High."

(4) And they said to the Lord of the ages:

'Lord of lords, God of gods,
King of kings, and God of all ages,[40]
the throne of Your glory stands
for all generations and all ages,
and Your name is holy and glorious
and blessed for all ages!'

(5) You have made all things,
and You have power over everything:
and all things are exposed
and open in Your sight,
and You see everything,
and nothing can hide itself from You.

(6) You see what Azazel has done,
he has taught all unrighteousness on earth
and revealed the eternal secrets
that were secured in heaven,
which men were striving to learn:

---

40 See Revelation 19:16. John also ascribes these titles to Jesus Christ.

(7) And Semjaza, to whom you have given authority
to rule over his associates.
(8) And they have gone to the daughters of men on the earth,
and have been intimate with women,
and have defiled themselves,
and taught them all kinds of sins.

(9) And the women have given birth to giants,
and the whole earth is now filled with blood
and unrighteousness because of it.

(10) And now, look!
The souls of those who have died
are crying out and making their suit
to the gates of heaven,
and their cries have ascended
and will not stop resounding
because of the lawless deeds
which are still happening on the earth.[41]

(11) And You know everything before it happens,
and You see these things
and You have allowed them,

---

41 See Genesis 4:10. The imagery presented in this chapter is similar to the way
that Genesis describes Abel's blood as "crying out" from the ground.

so why have You not yet directed us
to do anything for them?[42]

The Days of Noah Revealed

10 (1) Then the Most High,
the Great and Holy One spoke,
and sent Uriel to the son of Lamech,[43] saying:
(2) 'Go to Noah and tell him:

"Hide yourself in My Name!"[44]

And show him the end that is approaching:
that the whole earth will be destroyed,
for a flood is about to come upon the whole earth,
and it will destroy everything that is on it.[45]

(3) And now teach him so that he may escape
and so that his bloodline may be preserved for
all the generations of the world.'
(4) And then the Lord said to Raphael:

---

42 Note that even though the spirits of mankind appealed to the angels for help, the angels could not intervene until God *directed* them to do so in the following chapter.

43 The son of Lamech was Noah. See Genesis 5:28-32.

44 This command adds another layer of meaning to what Noah's ark represented: we also must "hide ourselves in the name of the Lord" to find refuge in times of trouble, just as Noah hid himself in the ark. See Proverbs 18:10.

45 See Genesis chapter 6 for a parallel to this chapter.

'Bind Azazel hand and foot,[46]
and cast him into the darkness:
and make an opening in the desert,
which is in Dudael, and cast him there.[47]

(5) And place upon him rough and jagged rocks,
and cover him with darkness,
and let him stay there forever,
and cover his face so he will see no light.
(6) And he will be thrown into the fire
on the day of the great judgment.[48]

[7] And heal the earth
which these angels have corrupted,
and declare that it will be restored,
and that its curse will be removed,[49]
so that not all of mankind will die
because of all of the occult things
that the Watchers have shared
and taught to their sons.

---

46 See Matthew 18:18-19.

47 See Matthew 12:43. Jesus explains that, "an unclean spirit goes through arid places seeking rest and does not find it."

48 See Matthew 25:42. Jesus explains that there is "an eternal fire prepared for the devil and his angels."

49 See Revelation 22:3.

(8) And the whole earth has been corrupted
through the works that were taught by Azazel:
[therefore], ascribe all sin to him.'

(9)And the Lord said to Gabriel:

'Go forth against those of mixed blood,
whose bloodline is corrupted,
and [march] against the children of fornication:
eradicate the children of fornication
and the children of the Watchers from humanity.
Cause them to march out against each other
so that they will destroy each other in battle
and not have long to live.

(10) And no request that their fathers make of you
will be granted for them;
for they hope to live an eternal life,
or [at least] that each one of them will
live five hundred years.'

(11) And the Lord said to Michael:[50]

'Go, bind Semjaza and his associates
who have been intimate with women

---

50 See Revelation 12:7-9. The archangel Michael made war against Satan in
heaven until he was cast down to the earth.

and who have defiled themselves with them
in all of their filthiness.

(12) And when their sons have killed each other,
and they have seen the destruction of their loved ones,
bind them securely for seventy generations
in the valleys of the earth,
until the day of their judgment
when they will waste away,
until the judgment that is forever and ever
is consummated.

(13) In those days they shall be
led off to the abyss of fire:
and to the torment and the prison
where they will be imprisoned forever.[51]
And whoever will be condemned and destroyed
will also be bound together with them[52]
from that time until the end of all generations.

(15) And destroy all the spirits of the corrupted
and the children of the Watchers,
because they have wronged mankind.
Remove all that is wrong
from the face of the earth
and let every evil work end:

---

51 See Revelation 9:1-2 for a parallel.

52 See Matthew 25:41.

and let the plant of righteousness and truth appear:
and it will certainly be a blessing;[53]
the works of righteousness and truth
will be planted in truth and joy forevermore.

(17) And then the righteous will escape,
and they will live until
they have thousands of children,
and they will live in peace for all of
the days of their youth and their old age.

(18) And then the whole earth
will be tilled in righteousness,
and it will all be planted with trees
and it will overflow with blessing.[54]
(19) And every desirable kind of tree
will be planted on it,
and they will plant vines on it
and the vine that they plant there
will yield abundant wine,
and as for all the seed which is sown on it
each measure of it will bear a thousand,

---

53 Compare this verse with Isaiah 53:1-2. This "plant" could refer to a pure and preserved Messianic bloodline. It may also refer to the olive branch that the dove brought back to Noah.

54 Note that this is another list of blessings, declared by Enoch for the righteous.

and each measure of olives
will yield ten presses of oil.[55]

(20) And cleanse the earth
from all of the effects of oppression,
and from all unrighteousness,
and from all sin,
and from all godlessness.
And purge the earth of all defilement.[56]

(21) And all of the children of men
will become righteous,
and all nations will offer to Me
their worship and adoration.[57]
And the earth will be cleansed
from all defilement,
and from all sin, and from all punishment,
and from all torment,
and I will never again allow these things
upon it from generation to generation
and forever.[58]

---

55 See Joel 2:19, 24.

56 See Zechariah 13:1-6.

57 See Zechariah chapter 14:16-21.

58 See Revelation 21:1-5.

11

(1) And in those days I will open
the storehouses of blessing
that are in the heaven,
and pour them out upon the earth
over all of the work and endeavors
of mankind.[59]

(2) And truth and peace will be companions[60]
throughout all the days of the world
and throughout all generations.'

Enoch Encounters the Watchers' Council

12

(1) Enoch was hidden before this happened,
and no man knew where he was,
or where he lived,
or what had become of him.

(2) But he was dealing with the Watchers,
and he spent his days with the holy angels.[61]

(3) And I, Enoch, was blessing the Lord of Majesty

---

59 See Malachi 3:8-12.

60 See Psalm 85:10, Zechariah 8:19.

61 Notice that Enoch dealt only briefly with these evil and demonic powers, but spent his days with the holy angels.

and the King of the Ages, when suddenly
the Watchers called to me—Enoch the scribe—and said:

(4) 'Enoch, you scribe of righteousness,
leave, come speak to the Watchers of heaven
who have left the high heaven,
the holy eternal place,
and have defiled themselves with women,
and have done what the children of the earth do,
and have chosen wives for themselves:

[Then Enoch replied:]

"You have brought great destruction upon the earth:
(5) And you will have no peace or forgiveness of sin:
and to the extent that you delight in your children,
(6) you will witness the murder of your beloved ones,
and will grieve over their destruction,
and even if you make a petition
from now until eternity,
you will never receive mercy and peace."'

13 (1) And Enoch went and said:
'Azazel, you will have no peace:
a severe sentence is decreed against you
to put you in chains:
(2) and you will not be tolerated
or have any request granted,

because you have taught unrighteousness,
and because of all of the works of godlessness

and unrighteousness and sin
which you have revealed to men.'
(3) Then I went and spoke to them all together,
and they were all afraid,
and were seized by fear and trembling.
(4) And they asked me to draw up a petition for them
so that they might find forgiveness,
and to read their petition
in the presence of the Lord of heaven.
(5) For from then on,
they could not speak with Him
or lift up their eyes to heaven
because of the shame
of their sins for which they had been condemned.

(6) Then I wrote out their petition:
a prayer concerning their spirits
and their individual deeds
and I included their requests to receive forgiveness
and length of days.

(7) And I went out and sat down
at the waters of Dan, in the land of Dan,
to the south and west of Hermon:
I read their petition until I fell asleep.

(8) And then a dream came to me,
and visions came upon me,
and I saw visions of rebuke,
and a voice came asking me

to speak to the sons of heaven,
and reprimand them.

(9) And when I woke up, I went to them
and they were all sitting together,
weeping in Abelsjail,
which is between Lebanon and Seneser,
with their faces covered.

(10) And I described to them all of the visions
which I had seen in my sleep,
and I began to speak the words of righteousness,
and to reprimand the Watchers of heaven.

A Vision of the New Jerusalem

14 (1) The book of the words of righteousness,
and the reprimand of the eternal Watchers
in accordance with the command
of the Great and Holy One in that vision.

(2) In my sleep, I saw what I will now say with my mortal
tongue and with the breath of my mouth:
these the Great One has given to men

so that they can have conversation
and understand with their hearts.

(3) Just as He has created [mankind] and given the power of
understanding the word of wisdom to man,
so He has also created me and given me the power
to rebuke the Watchers, the children of heaven.

(4) I wrote out your petition,
but in my vision it was made clear
that your petition will not be accepted
throughout all the days of eternity.
And this is the final judgment:
your petition is denied.

(5) You shall not ascend into heaven
again for all eternity,
and the decree has gone out
to restrict you to the earth
for all of the days of the world.[62]

(6) It was already decreed that you will
see the destruction of your beloved sons
and that you will have no pleasure in them,
but you will see them fall by the sword.

---

62 See Ephesians 6:12, Revelation chapter 12.

(7) And your petition for [your sons]
will [also] be denied, even if you ask it yourselves:
even though you weep and beg and repeat
all of the words contained in what I have written.

(8) The vision was shown to me like this:
In the vision, I watched
as the clouds invited me,[63]
and a mist summoned me,
and the course of the stars
and the lightnings sped and hastened me,
and the winds in the vision caused me to fly
and lifted me upward,
and bore me into heaven.[64]

(9) And I went in until I came near a wall
which was made of crystals
and surrounded by tongues of fire:
and it began to terrify me.

---

63 These are far more than ordinary clouds: it was the very glory of God Himself
that was inviting Enoch into the heavens. The Scriptures often describe the clouds
of God's presence, power, and glory that surround Him (see Psalm 18:11-12,
Psalm 68:4, Psalm 97:2). Likewise, Ezekiel and Daniel both describe the day of
the Lord as a "day of clouds" (see Ezekiel 30:3, Daniel 7:13). Even Christ Himself
described Himself returning again on the same clouds of "power and glory" that
He rode up into heaven when He ascended (see Matthew 24:30 and Matthew
26:64).

64 See Ezekiel 8:3-4, where Ezekiel was similarly lifted up.

[10] And I went into the tongues of fire
and approached a large house
which was made of crystals:
and the walls of the house
were like a tessellated floor (made) of crystals,[65]
and its foundation was also made of crystal.[66]

(11) Its ceiling was like the path
of the stars and the lightnings,
and between them were fiery cherubim,
and their heaven was as clear as water.
(12) A flaming fire surrounded the walls,
and its portals blazed with fire.

(13) And I entered into that house,
and it was hot as fire and cold as ice:
there were none of this life's delights there:
fear covered me, and trembling got hold upon me.
(14) And as I shook and trembled, I fell on my face.

------

65 A tessellated floor is a floor that uses tiles to create geometric patterns. These
were common throughout the civilized world in ancient times.

66 See Revelation 21:9-27. Enoch's description of the former and latter "crystal
houses" is very similar to the description of the New Jerusalem in Revelation.
(Both include crystal foundations, crystal stones, and a "great, high wall.")

(15) And I beheld a vision,
and suddenly there was a second house,
greater than the former,[67]
and the entire portal stood open before me,
and it was made of flames of fire.

(16) And in every respect it so far exceeded
[the former house] in splendor
and magnificence and magnitude
that I cannot even describe to you
its splendor and its overwhelming brilliance.

(17) And its floor was made of fire,
and above it were lightnings
and the path of the stars,
and its ceiling was also flaming fire.

(18) And I looked and saw there a lofty throne:
its appearance was like crystal,
and the wheels were like the shining sun,[68]
and there was the vision of cherubim.

(19) And from underneath the throne
came streams of flaming fire
so powerful that I couldn't even look at them.

---

67 See the parallel text in Haggai 2:9.

68 See Ezekiel 1, Daniel 7.

(20) And the Great Glory sat on it,
and His garment shone
more brightly than the sun
and was whiter than any snow.[69]

(21) None of the angels could even enter
and they could not gaze upon His face
because of His magnificence and glory
and no flesh could behold Him.

(22) There was a flaming fire all around Him,
and a great fire stood before Him,[70]
and none around could draw near to Him:
ten thousand times ten thousand
stood before Him,
but He needed no counselor.

(23) And the most holy ones
who were near Him
did not leave by night
or withdraw from His Presence.[71]

---

69 See Revelation 1:9-17. This appears to be an encounter with the eternal and living Christ, who is described in a very similar way in the Book of Revelation.

70 See Revelation 4, Daniel 7.

71 These who "never leave Him or withdraw from Him" could refer to the generation that is described in Revelation chapter seven who are "standing around the throne" and "serve Him day and night in His temple." This is our highest purpose. See Revelation chapter 7.

(24) Until then, I had been prostrate
on my face and trembling[72]
but then, the Lord called me
and he spoke to me with His own voice:

'Come here, Enoch,
and hear my word.'[73]

(25) And one of the holy ones
came to me and woke me up,
and He made me rise up
and approach the door [74]
and I bowed my face to the ground.

A Verdict Against the Watchers

15 (1) And I heard His voice answer and tell me:
'Fear not, Enoch,[75]
you are a righteous man

---

72 See Revelation 1:17-18, where John encounters the Living Christ in a very similar manner.

73 See Revelation 4:1, where John is beckoned, "Come up here, and I will show you what must take place after this."

74 There is also an open door in Revelation 4:1.

75 In the Scriptures, prophets and great men of God are usually terrified when they encounter angels clothed in great power and glory. You'll find the command to "fear not" is part of nearly every prophetic commission in the Bible.

and a scribe of righteousness[76]:
come near me and hear my voice.

(2) And go, say to the Watchers of heaven,
who have sent you to intercede for them:
"You should intercede for men,
and not men for you:

(3) Why have you left
the high, holy, and eternal heaven,
and slept with women,
and defiled yourselves
with the daughters of men
and taken wives for yourselves,
and behaved like the children of the earth,
and sired giants as your sons?

(4) Even though you were holy, spiritual,
and living the eternal life,
you have defiled yourselves
with the blood of women,
and have sired children with flesh and blood,
and, as the children of men,
have lusted after flesh and blood
just like [men] who die and perish.

---

76 The title of scribe is critical to understanding Enoch's purpose. It was important for him to write down the revelations he received so future generations could
read them when they were needed.

(5) I have given wives [only] to men
that they might impregnate them,
and have children with them,
so that they will lack nothing on earth.

(6) However, you were formerly spiritual,
living the eternal life, and immortal
for all generations of the world.

(7) I have not appointed any wives for you
because the spiritual beings of heaven
must remain in the heavenly realms.

(8) And now, these giants,
who have been produced from spirits and flesh,
will become evil spirits upon the earth,
and the earth will be their only dwelling.

(9) Evil spirits have proceeded from their bodies;
Even though they were born of men,
their seed and their beginning
is from the holy Watchers;
so now they will only be evil spirits on earth,
and they will be called evil spirits.[77]

---

77 This verse clarifies the difference between fallen angels and evil spirits. Evil spirits are also referred to as demons.

(10) [Now], the spirits of heaven
will continue to dwell in heaven,
but the spirits of the earth
which were born upon the earth
will be confined to living only on the earth.

(11) And the spirits of the giants afflict,
oppress, destroy, attack, do battle,
and work destruction on the earth,
and cause trouble:[78]
they take no food,
but nevertheless hunger and thirst,
and cause offenses.

And these spirits will rise up
against the children of men and against women,
because they proceeded from them.[79]

16 (1) Beginning with the days of the slaughter,
destruction, and death of the giants,
the [evil] spirits that come from their flesh
will destroy without facing judgment--
so they will destroy until the day they are annihilated,
at the great judgment in which

---

78 See John 10:10.

79 See Genesis 3:14-15 and Revelation 12. Note that the war between "the seed
of the woman" and the "seed of the serpent" began in the Book of Genesis continues in the Book of Revelation.

the age itself will be finished,
then the Watchers and the godless
will be completely terminated.

(2) And now as to the Watchers
who have sent you to intercede for them,
who were previously in heaven, tell them:

[3] "You have been in heaven,
but all of the mysteries
were not revealed to you,[80]
and you knew only the worthless ones,
because you have hard hearts,
you have made these known to the women,
and through these mysteries
women and men work much evil on earth."

(4) Therefore, tell them: "You have no peace."'

---

80 See 1 Corinthians 2:8-10 and Isaiah 52:15. There is ample evidence in Scripture to suggest that Satan, fallen angels, and evil spirits never foresaw what Christ would accomplish on the cross or what His saints would become and accomplish through the power of His blood. There may also be many other mysteries that the enemy of our souls does not know yet.

Enoch's Journey Through Earth and Sheol

CHAPTERS 17-36

Places of Power, Authority, and Banishment

17
(1) And I was taken and carried to a place in which the attendants were all blazing flames of fire, but they appeared as men when they wished.[81]

(2) And they brought me
to a place of great darkness,
and to a mountain whose summit
rose all the way up to heaven.

(3) And I saw the positions of the stars
and the treasuries from which stars
and peals of thunder emerge.
And in the outermost depths,
I saw a bow and a quiver of arrows
which were all made of brilliant blazing fire,
and a sword made of resplendent lightnings.[82]

---

81 Psalm 104:4 explains the characteristics of His holy angels: "He makes winds His messengers, flames of fire His servants."

82 This entire chapter is remarkably similar to II Samuel 22:10-16 and Psalm 18, which use similar imagery to describe the power and glory that emerges from God's Presence when He intervenes on our behalf. The weapons described here might also imply that this is "God's armory" on the outer reaches of the universe.

(4) And they took me to the living waters,
and to the fire of the west,
which receives every setting sun.
(5) And I came to a river of fire
in which the fire flows like water
and flows into the great sea towards the west.[83]

(6) I saw the great rivers
and came to the great river
and to the great darkness,
and went to the realm
where no flesh walks.

(7) I saw the mountains of the darkness of winter
and the source of the fountains of the deep.
(8) I saw the mouths of all the rivers of the earth
and the mouth of the deep.

18 (1) I observed the storehouses of all the winds: I
saw how He had used them
to set up the whole creation
and establish the earth's solid foundation.

(2) And I saw the cornerstone of the earth:
I saw the four winds that ferry the earth
and import the atmosphere of heaven.
(3) And I saw how the winds

---

83 See Daniel 7:10.

expand the canopies of heaven,
and have their station between heaven and earth:
these are the shafts of heaven.
(4) I saw the winds of heaven which turn
and bring the circumference of the sun
and all the stars to their setting.
(5) I saw the winds on the earth
which carry the clouds:
I saw the paths of the angels.
At the end of the earth,
I saw the canopy of heaven
that stretched out above it.[84]

[6] From there, I continued on until
I saw a place which burns day and night,
where there are seven mountains
of magnificent stones,
three towards the east,
and three towards the south.

(7) And as for those towards the east,
one was made of colored stone,
and one was made of pearl,[85]

---

84 Verses 3-5 are describing both natural processes and angelic activity. This chapter describes interaction between heaven and earth—or the "spirit realm" and the "earthly realm."

85 See Revelation 21:21, the gates of the New Jerusalem are also made of pearl.

and one was made of jacinth,[86]
and those towards the south
were made of red stone.[87]

(8) But the middle one reached to heaven
like the throne of God, of alabaster, and
the summit of the throne was of sapphire.[88]

(9) And I saw a flaming fire.
And beyond these mountains
(10) is a region at the end of the earth:
and there the heavens were completed.

(11) And I saw a deep abyss,
with shafts of heavenly fire,
and among them I saw columns of fire
which were continually falling,
which went far beyond what anyone could measure
in both their height and their depth.[89]

(12) And beyond that abyss
I saw a place which had

---

86 Jacinth is a red transparent gemstone and a variety of zircon. It was used in the twelve stones of the priestly ephod and is also one of the stones composing the structure of the New Jerusalem. See Exodus 28:15-21 and Revelation 21:20.

87 The mountains of Sinai were also red in appearance.

88 See Exodus 24:9-11 for a parallel.

89 See Revelation 9:1-2 and Revelation 20:1-3.

no firmament of the heaven above,
and no firmly founded earth beneath it:
there was no water upon it, and no birds,
but it was a waste and horrible place.

(13) I saw there seven stars
like great burning mountains,
And when I asked about them,
(14) the angel said:
'This place is the end of heaven and earth:
this has become a prison for the stars
and the host of heaven.[90]

(15) And the stars which roll over the edge
and into the fire are the ones which rebelled
against God's command when they first arose,
because they did not come forth
at their appointed times.

(16) And in His wrath,
He bound them here
until the time when their guilt
will be consummated,
even for ten thousand years.'[91]

---

90 Stars here signify fallen angels. See Revelation 12:4.

91 See Revelation 20:2.

19

(1) And Uriel said to me:
'The angels who have been
intimate with women
will remain here, and their spirits
will take on many different forms
in order to defile mankind
and deceive them into making sacrifices to demons,[92]
while believing that they are gods,
they will remain here until
the great judgment day
when they will be judged
and totally annihilated.'

(2) And the wives of the angels
who went astray will become tempting spirits.' [93]
(3) And it was only I, Enoch, who saw the vision
of where everything ends:
no one else saw what I did.

---

92 See I Corinthians 10:20.

93 Or sirens.

Archangels Who Watch Over Mankind

20
(1) And these are the names of the holy archangels who watch:[94]

(2) Uriel, one of the holy archangels,[95]
he stretches his covering over the world
and stands above the great chasm.

(3) Raphael, one of the holy archangels,[96]
he provides a canopy for the spirits of men.

(4) Raguel, one of the holy archangels,[97]
he is an avenger of the galaxies.

(5) Michael, one of the holy archangels,[98]
he is unique because he stretches

---

94 Knowing an angel's name is biblical: The Bible specifically lists Michael and Gabriel by name several times. In some Christian denominations, those who name angels are accused of worshipping them. It is true that angels often warned people against worshipping them (see Revelation 22:8-9). However, the Scriptures never warn us against knowing the names of heavenly beings. In fact, it often names them for us.

95 Uriel means "God is my light." Note that the name of each angel is connected to his unique mandate from God. This is why knowing an angel's name can be helpful.

96 Raphael means "God has healed."

97 Raguel means "Friend of God."

98 Michael means "One like God."

his covering over the greatest champions
from among mankind and he has authority over chaos.

(6) Saraqael, one of the holy archangels,[99]
he has dominion over the evil spirits.

(7) Gabriel, one of the holy archangels,[100]
he stretches his canopy over Paradise
and over the serpents and the Cherubim.

(8) Remiel, one of the holy archangels,[101]
God has made him to provide a canopy
for those who rise.

The Fiery Abyss

21 (1) And I continued until I reached a place
where everything was in complete chaos.
(2) And I saw something
that absolutely horrified me:
there was no heaven above
and no firmly founded earth,

---

99 Saraqael means "Command of God."

100 Gabriel means "Strongman of God."

101 Remiel means "Mercy of God."

it was a place of complete chaos and horror.[102]
(3) And there I saw seven stars of the heaven
bound together in it, like great mountains
and burning with fire.

(4) Then I said:
'For what sin are they bound,
and why have they been thrown in here?'

(5) Then Uriel, one of the holy archangels who was with me
and who ruled over them, said:

'Enoch, why do you ask this,
and why are you eager for the truth?
(6) These are of the number of the stars of heaven
that have disobeyed what the Lord has commanded,[103]
and [they] are bound here for ten thousand years,
the time demanded by their sins, are completed.'

(7) And then I went to another place,
which was still more horrible than the first,
and I saw a sight that filled me with horror:
there was a great fire which burned and blazed,

---

102 See Genesis 1:2 for comparison. The Hebrew word that is translated as
"formless and empty" may also be translated as complete chaos. Also, Jesus referred
multiple times to the "outer darkness" where there will be "weeping and gnashing
of teeth" (see Matthew 22:13, Matthew 25:30).

103 Jude alludes to this chapter in Jude 1:6. Read all of Jude for a clear comparison to this chapter.

and the ground was broken
and ruptured as far as the abyss,
being full of great descending columns of fire:

I could not see its full magnitude
and I could not imagine its full extent.

(8) Then I said: 'How fearful is this place
and how terrible to look upon!'

(9) Then Uriel, one of the holy archangels
who was with me, answered me and asked:
'Enoch, why do you have such fear and terror?'

And I answered:
'Because of this fearful place,
and because of this spectacle of great pain.'

(10) And he said to me:
'This place is the prison of the angels,
and here they will be imprisoned forever.'

A Vision of Sheol

22 (1) From there I went to another place,
and He showed me in the west
another great and lofty mountain
of hard rock.
(2) [g] And there were four hollow chambers in it,

all of them were deep and had a polished surface:
three were dark, but one was bright
and there was a fountain of water in it.
And I said:

'These hollow places are smooth
and they look deep and dark.'[104]

(3) Then Raphael, one of the holy archangels
who was with me, answered:

'These hollow places have been
created for a specific purpose:
so that the spirits of the souls
of those who have died
may be gathered here,
until all the souls of mankind
are assembled here.[105]

(4) These places have been made to hold them
until the day when they will be judged

---

104 The [g] signifies that this verse is based on the Greek manuscript, which is
slightly different from the Ethiopian manuscript for this verse.

105 This is a description of what is referred to as Sheol throughout the Old
Testament. It was a "holding place" for both the righteous and unrighteous until
the judgment. When Christ died on the cross, all of the righteous were released
from this place and given access to the heavenly realms because His shed blood
removed the curse of sin and death from all who looked forward to His redemption (see Matthew 27:50-54, Luke 16:19-31).

and until the appointed time when
great judgment will come upon them.

(5) [g] I saw the spirit of a dead man
that was crying out for justice,
and his voice appealed to heaven for justice.

(6) And I asked Raphael, the angel who was with me:
'Who is this spirit which presents his case?
Whose voice appeals to heaven for justice?'

(7) And he explained to me:
'This is the spirit of Abel,
who was murdered by his brother Cain,
and he will continue to present his case against him
until all of his children are removed
from the face of the earth,
and until his seed is annihilated
from all of the bloodlines of men.'[106]

(8) [g]. Then I asked about all of these hollow places:
'Why is one separated from the other?'

(9) [g]. And he answered:
'These three have been made so that
the spirits of the dead can be separated.
And a section has been set apart

---

106 See Genesis 4:10 and Hebrews 12:24 for biblical parallels to this chapter.

for the spirits of the righteous,
in which there is a spring of water
that shines with radiant light.
(10) [g]. And another section
has been made for sinners
who die and are buried in the earth,
but judgment was never executed
upon them in their lifetime.
(11) [g] Here their spirits will reside
in isolation and in great pain,
until the great day of judgment,
these cursed ones will be punished
and tormented forever,
so that there will be retribution for their spirits.
He will confine them there forever.

(12) [g] And another section has been made
for the spirits of those who cry out for justice,
they are continually declaring
how they were murdered,
as well as the circumstances of their deaths
during the days of great wickedness.

(13) [g] And this section has been made
for the spirits of men who are not righteous,
but are sinners who rejected God,
and they will be companions of the lawless [ones]:
but their spirits will not be punished

in the day of judgment because they
will not be raised up to leave from here.

(14) [g] Then I blessed the Lord of Glory, saying:

'Blessed are You,
Lord of Righteousness,
who rules over all the world.'

The Abyss Revisited

23 (1) From there I went to another place
to the west of the ends of the earth.
(2) And I saw a burning fire
which flowed without resting,
and it never stopped its course day or night
because it flowed continually.

(3) And I asked: 'What is this which never rests?'

(4) Then Raguel, one of the holy archangels who was with
me, answered me, saying:

'This course of fire that you have seen
is the fire in the west which expels
all the luminaries of heaven.'

The Fiery Mountains and the Tree of Life

24

(1) From there I went to another place of the earth, and he showed me a mountain range made of fire which burned day and night.

(2) And I went beyond it and I saw
seven magnificent mountains
which were all unique and different,
and their stones were magnificent and beautiful,
together they were completely captivating,
of glorious appearance with a perfect exterior:
three were towards the east,
with each one established upon the others,
and three were towards the south,
with each one established upon the others,
and [yet there were] deep rough ravines
that made them separate and distinct.

(3) And the seventh mountain
was in the middle of these,
and it far excelled the others in height,
it looked like the seat of a throne
and fragrant trees encircled the throne.

(4) And among them was a tree
unlike anything I have ever smelled,
there is truly no other tree like it:

it had a fragrance that surpassed all other fragrances,
and its leaves and blooms and wood
will never wither or rot,
and its fruit is beautiful,
resembling the dates of a palm.

(5) Then I said:
'How beautiful and fragrant is this tree,

and its leaves are lovely,
and its blooms look delightful.'

(6) Then Michael, who was one of the holy and honored archangels with me and was their captain, spoke to me.

25 (1) And [Michael] said to me:
'Enoch, why do you ask me
about this tree's fragrance,
and why do you want to learn the truth [about it]?'

[2] Then I replied:
'I want to know about everything,
but especially about this tree.'

[3] And he answered me, saying:
'This high mountain which you have seen,
whose summit is like the throne of God,
is His throne, where the Great and Holy One,
the Lord of Glory, the Eternal King,

will sit when He comes down
to inhabit the earth with goodness.[107]

(4) And as for this fragrant tree, no mortal
is allowed to touch it until the great judgment,
when He will take vengeance on all
and bring everything to its eternal perfection.
Then, it will be given to the righteous and holy.

(5) Its fruit will nourish the elect:
it will be transplanted to the holy place,
to the temple of the Lord, the Eternal King.[108]

(6) Then they will overflow with joy and gladness,
and they will enter the holy place,
and its fragrance will reside in their very bones.[109]
Because of this, they will live a long life on earth,
just as your fathers lived.

---

107 Revelation 21:10 refers to a "great and high mountain" upon which the New
Jerusalem will come to rest when it descends from heaven. Note that John also
explains that at this time, "the dwelling of God will be with men" (see Revelation
21:3).

108 See Revelation 22:2, which also describes the tree of life being planted where
the New Jerusalem will descend.

109 When we enter into communion with the Spirit of Christ, our very bones
are infused with His intoxicating fragrance. He gives life, light, and love to every
aspect of our being when we feast upon His Presence.

And in their days no sorrow or plague
or torment or calamity will be able to touch them.'[110]

(7) Then I blessed the God of Glory,
the Eternal King,
who has prepared these wonderful things
for the righteous,
and has created them
and promised to give [these blessings] to them.

26

(1) And I went from there
to the middle of the earth,
and I saw a blessed place[111]
in which there were trees
with branches grafted [into] and blooming
from a dismembered tree.[112]

(2) And there I saw a holy mountain,
and underneath the mountain
to the east there was a stream and it flowed towards the
south.[113]

---

110 Revelation 21:4 uses similar language: "There will be no more mourning or death or crying or pain, because the old order of things has passed away."

111 In this chapter, Enoch describes the landscape of Jerusalem and the surrounding area before it was inhabited.

112 See Isaiah 11:1, Romans 11:11-24, and John 15:1-17.

113 See Ezekiel 47. Ezekiel also saw a river that was "toward the east" and "flowed from the south side."

(3) And I saw towards the east
another mountain higher than this,
and between them a deep and narrow ravine:
in it a stream also ran underneath the mountain.

(4) And to the west,
there was another mountain,
of a much lower elevation,
and a deep and dry ravine between them:
and another deep and dry ravine
was at the bottom of the three mountains.

(5) And all the ravines were deep and narrow,
being formed of hard rock,
and trees were not planted upon them.

(6) And I marveled at the rocks,
and I marveled at the ravine,
and I was filled with awe.[114]

---

114 Notice Enoch's sense of awe and wonder here. He is marveling at rocks, even
after seeing a vast house made of crystal and fire.

The Valley of Gehenna

27
(1) Then I said:
'What is the purpose of this blessed land,
which is entirely filled with trees,
and this cursed valley between it?'[115]

(2) Then Uriel, one of the holy archangels
who was with me, answered:

'This cursed valley is for
those who are forever cursed:
Here all the cursed will be gathered together,
those who speak blasphemous words
against the Lord with their lips
and insult His glory.
[g] Here they will be gathered together,
and this is where they will live.

(3) In the days of that final age,
true judgment will reside in
the presence of the righteous forever:

---

115 This most likely refers to the Valley of Gehenna. Gehenna is the word that
Jesus used to refer to hell in Matthew 5:22, Matthew 5:30, Matthew 10:28, and
Matthew 23:33. During the time of Christ, all of the garbage—and even dead
bodies—were gathered and burned here and its smoke rose continually.

and here the godly will exalt the Lord of Glory,[116]
the Eternal King.[117]

(4) In the days of judgment over the former,
they will bless Him for his mercy according
to the full measure of mercy they were shown.[118]

(5) Then I blessed the Lord of Glory
and radiated His glory
and gloriously shouted His praise.

Visions of a Blessed Land

28 (1) From there, I went towards the east,
into the midst of the mountain range
in the desert, and I saw a wilderness
and it was solitary, full of trees and plants.

(2) And water gushed forth from above,[119]

(3) rushing like river rapids

---

116 There is an interesting parallel here. First, the wicked are confined here
because they cursed God. Then, it becomes a place where all those who are shown
mercy will praise God. There is a mystery here which needs to be more fully
explored.

117 This term "eternal kin" most likely refers to Christ who is the "Lord of Glory"
and whom the Bible describes as "our brother" (see Romans 8:29).

118 See Luke 7:37.

119 See Isaiah 35.

towards the northwest and clouds
and dew ascended from its banks.

29

(1) Then I went to another place
in the desert, and drew near to the east
of this mountain range.

(2) And there I saw aromatic trees exhaling
the [intoxicating] fragrance of frankincense and myrrh.
These trees were similar to the almond tree.[120]

30

(1) And beyond these,
I went far to the east,
and I saw another place,
a valley [full] of water.

(2) And in it was a tree,
with the essence of fragrant trees
such as the mastic.

(3) And on the sides of those valleys
I saw fragrant cinnamon.[121]

---

120 Frankincense and myrrh are both highly aromatic tree resins. They appear throughout the Bible and usually represent the fragrance of Christ. This is worth exploring on your own, from their use in the Levitical priesthood, to the gifts of the Magi at Christ's birth, and to their use at His preparation for burial.

121 Cinnamon is derived from the inner bark of the tree. It was also used in the sacred anointing oil that consecrated the Levitical priesthood (see Exodus 30:22-33).

And beyond these I proceeded to the east.[122]

31

(1) And I saw other mountains,
and among them were groves of trees,
and sweet nectars flowed out from them,
which are called sarara and galbanum.[123]

(2) And beyond these mountains
I saw another mountain
to the east of the ends of the earth,
upon which there were aloe trees,

and all the trees were full of stacte,[124]
because they were like almond trees.

(3) And when one burned it,
it smelled sweeter than any other fragrance [on earth].

---

122 These chapters could be interpreted as journeys through the Promised Land before it was inhabited, in which God allowed Enoch to see where His covenant would be established. However, these could also refer to places in the realm of the Spirit. Many of those who have walked the "thin gold line" have smelled all manner of fragrances while communing with the Lord (see II Corinthians 2:14-15).

123 These are aromatic gum resins which were used in making the incense that burned on the altar of incense before the gateway to the Ark of the Covenant.

124 This was also used in the priestly incense described in Exodus chapter 30.

Eden and the Tree of Knowledge

32

(1) [g] To the northeast
I saw seven mountains
full of precious nard and mastic
and cinnamon and pepper.

(2) And then I flew over
the summits of all of these mountains,
far towards the east of the earth,
and flew above the Erythraean sea
and I traveled far from it,
until I flew over the angel Zotiel.[125]

(3) [e] And I came to the
Garden of Righteousness,
and saw beyond those trees
many large trees growing there
which had a beautiful fragrance:
They were large,
very beautiful and glorious,

---

125 Zotiel means "little one of God." He may be one of the angelic guardians of
Eden based on the next verse in the chapter.

and [then I saw] the tree of *knowledge* [126]
through eating it they
come to know great *knowledge*.

(4) That tree is as tall as a fir,
and its leaves are like Carob tree leaves:
and its fruit appears in clusters like grapes
and it is very beautiful. [127]
And the fragrance of the tree
penetrates the air for miles around.

(5) Then I said:
'How beautiful is this tree,
and how attractive it looks!'

(6) Then Raphael, the holy archangel
who was with me, answered:
'This is the tree of *knowledge*,
and your ancient father and mother
who came before you
ate of it and gained *knowledge*
and their eyes were opened,

---

126 The words in this particular chapter that are translated as knowledge and italicized were all rendered as wisdom in the 1912 translation by R.H. Charles. Many have considered these words to be synonyms; however, I consider the word knowledge to be a more accurate reflection of the spiritual reality of this passage, because it aligns closely with Genesis chapters 2 and 3. Even if these words remained rendered as wisdom, it could be supported by Eve's words in Genesis 3:6.

127 See Genesis 3:6.

and they knew that they were naked
and they were driven out of the garden.'

33

(1) From that place, I went
to the ends of the earth
and saw very large animals there,
and every one was unique;
and I saw birds which were all different
in appearance and beauty,
and they all had different songs[128]

(2) And to the east of those creatures
I saw the ends of the earth
where heaven meets earth,
and the portals of heaven opened.[129]

(3) And I saw how the stars of heaven come out,
and I counted the portals out of which they proceed,[130]
and wrote down all of the channels
of each individual star by itself,
according to their number and their names,

---

128 The prophet, Bob Jones, often described the "songbirds" of heaven when he was among us.

129 The concept of heavenly portals is biblical. The best example is in Genesis 28, when Jacob declares that Bethel is "none other than the house of God, the gateway to heaven." The Hebrew word for gateway may also be translated portal. However, there are many other examples in Scripture of heaven "opening" to release blessing or angelic activity on the earth.

130 This could speak of "angelic portals," one of which Jacob saw in Genesis 28.

their courses and their positions,
and their times and their months,
as Uriel the holy angel who was with me showed me.[131]

(4) He showed all things to me
and wrote them down for me:
also he wrote down their names for me,
the laws by which they operate,
and their companies.[132]

Portals of Blessing and Glory

34 (1) From there, I went towards the north
to the ends of the earth,
and there I saw
a great and glorious machine[133]
at the ends of the whole earth.

(2) And here I saw
three portals of heaven

---

131 This text is not an endorsement of astrology, which is a pagan practice.
Rather, it is a call to develop a deeper prophetic understanding of how angels operate and move from one dimension to another in performing God's will. One lesson that can be gleaned from this particular chapter is that angels, like the stars of heaven, all have a specific place where they belong in heaven and a specific purpose to fulfill as they fill that position.

132 Fallen angels are now marked by darkness and chaos. But God's holy angels still operate with divine order, total alignment, and heavenly organization.

133 R.H. Charles translated this word as device.

open in the sky:
north winds blew through each one of them.[134]
And when they blow,
there is cold, hail, frost,
snow, dew, and rain.[135]

(3) They only blow for good out of one portal:
when they blow through the other two portals,
they strike the earth with destruction and catastrophe,
because they blow violently.

35 (1) And from there,
I went towards the west
to the ends of the earth,
and saw three portals of heaven open there
like what I had seen in the east,
the same number of portals,
and the same number of outlets.

36 (1) And from there,
I went to the south
to the ends of the earth,
and saw three open portals of heaven there:

---

134 Jeremiah 10:13 and Jeremiah 51:16 speak of the "storehouses of the wind"—a similar image to this one.

135 This could suggest that weather often aligns with what's happening in the unseen realm of the Spirit, a possibility that is worth exploring in the Scriptures, where Elijah commanded that it not rain until he said it would and Jesus calmed the storms.

and out of them came dew, rain, and wind.
(2) And from there, I went to the east
to the ends of the heaven,
and saw here the three eastern
portals of heaven open
and small portals above them.

(3) The stars of heaven go through
each one of these small portals
as they travel and run their course to the west
on the path which is shown to them.[136]

(4) And for as long as I saw this,
I continually showered my affection
on the Lord of Glory,
and I continued to bless the Lord of Glory
who has created all of these
magnificent and awesome wonders,
to show the greatness of His work
to the angels and to spirits and to men,
that they might appreciate
His handiwork and all of His creation:
that they might see how His creation
demonstrates His infinite power
and recognize this great work of His hands
and shower affection on Him forever.

----

136 We do not yet fully understand how angels and stars are connected, but it is a
connection in the Scriptures that goes beyond metaphor and symbolism. In some
sense, angels are stars from the Hebrew perspective. They are alike in that both
angels and stars are like flaming balls of fire that are too powerful and large for us
to fathom.

The Prophecies
(Also Known As "The Parables")

CHAPTER 37

Enoch Speaks to the Past and the Future

37 (1) Now this is the second vision that he saw, and it is a vision of wisdom—
which Enoch, the son of Jared,
the son of Mahalalel, the son of Cainan,
the son of Enos, the son of Seth, the son of Adam, saw.

(2) This is the beginning of the words of wisdom
that I spoke when I began to shout
to everyone who lives on the earth:

Hear, you men of ancient times,
and see, you who will come in the future,
the words of the Holy One which I will speak
in the Presence of the Lord of Spirits.[137]

(3) It was easier to declare this
to the men who lived in ancient times,
but we will not withhold
the impartation of wisdom
even from those who will come in the future.[138]

---

137 This title is similar to the title "Lord of lords" from Revelation 19:16. It emphasizes the dominion of God over every created spiritual entity: angels, demons, etc. It may also be compared to the name "Father of lights" (see James 1:17).

138 Enoch may have said that it was "easier" to preach his message to those who lived in ancient times because he lived among these ancient people. However, in order to preach to a future generation, he would (presumably) have to transcend time and space by the Spirit's power, a much more difficult proposition.

4) Until now, this magnitude of wisdom
has never been given by the Lord of Spirits,
yet I have received it based on my ability to see,[139]
because of the good pleasure of the Lord of Spirits,
who has given me eternal life.[140]

(5) Now three prophecies were imparted to me,
and I shouted them out as I proclaimed them [141]
to everyone who lives on earth.

---

139 See Ephesians 1:17. Paul speaks of a "spirit of wisdom and revelation." True wisdom is a gift from God and comes as a form of revelation from God.

140 Note that Enoch describes eternal life as a gift. This is a New Covenant concept (see Romans 6:23).

141 This shouting, which R.H. Charles translates as a "raised voice" could refer to simple shouting, but there is something supernatural about this if everyone in the earth could hear it and at different times (as is also described in verse 2). He may have had the volume and power of his voice supernaturally expanded, such as many revivalists who walked the thin gold line experienced. For example, George Whitefield could be heard preaching for many miles away as if he were right next to you. It could also refer to the fact that his message would resonate in the realm of the Spirit until everything he said came to fruition.

The First Prophecy

CHAPTERS 38-44

A Season of Holiness and Rising Glory

38

(1) The First Prophecy:
When the congregation
of the righteous appears,
and sinners are judged for their sins,
and they are driven from the face of the earth: [142]

(2) And when the Righteous One reveals Himself
before the eyes of the righteous,
to everyone who allowed their deeds
to be divinely orchestrated
and completely dependent upon
the Lord of Spirits,
and when the righteous see the light [143]
and [it shines from] the chosen ones
who live on the earth:

At that time, where will sinners make their home,
and where will the people who have rejected
the Lord of Spirits find rest?

---

142 This obviously points to the second coming of Christ, the promise of His coming is among the greatest blessings for our generation (see II Thessalonians 4, Revelation 19:11-21).

143 See Psalm 97:11.

It would have been better for them
if they had not been born.[144]
(3) When the secrets of the self-righteous
are revealed and sinners are judged,[145]
and the godless are driven away from
the presence of the righteous and chosen:
(4) From that time on, those that
exercise dominion over the earth
will no longer be powerful and exalted:[146]
In fact, they will not even be able to
look at the faces of the holy [people],
because the Lord of Spirits
will cause His light to radiate from
the faces of the holy, righteous, and elect.[147]

(5) Then the kings and
the powerful ones will perish
and will be surrendered into the hands
of the righteous and holy.[148]

---

144 Jesus uses these exact words in Matthew 26:24 and Mark 14:21. While He does not specifically cite Enoch in using these words, He shares this sentence within the context of discussing judgment—a judgment that this chapter clearly illuminates.

145 See Luke 12:1-3.

146 Note this chapter parallels Daniel 2: The kingdom of God will "increase and fill the earth," while the kingdoms of this world will quickly lose their power, authority, and dominion.

147 See Daniel 12:3 and Matthew 13:43.

148 See Psalm 2.

(6) And from then on,
none of them will ask for mercy anymore
from the Lord of Spirits because
their lives will be ended once and for all.[149]

Enoch Sees Houses of Prayer

39 (1) And in those days, this will happen:
children who are holy and elect
will descend from the highest heaven,
and their seed will become one
with the children of men.[150]

(2) And in those days,
Enoch received books of zeal and wrath,
and books of foreboding and banishment.
And mercy will not be given to them,
says the Lord of Spirits.

---

149 This most likely refers to the "second death" in the lake of fire at the end of age (see Revelation 20:14).

150 Verses one and two seem to refer back to the unrighteous union of fallen angels and men before the flood. However, in context, these verses actually refer to something that will happen at the end of the age (i.e. "at that time..."). Perhaps this is why Jesus warned that the end of the age would be similar to the "days of Noah" (see Matthew 24:37).

(3) And at that time, a whirlwind
carried me up and away from the earth,[151]
and set me down at the end of the heavens.

(4) And there I saw another vision,
of the houses of holy [people],
and the resting places of the righteous.
(5) Here I saw with my own eyes
that they lived alongside His righteous angels,
and their resting place was with the holy.
And they petitioned and interceded
and prayed for the children of men,
and righteousness flowed from them like water,
and mercy like fresh dew upon the earth:
This is how it will be with them forever and ever.[152]

(6a) And in that place, I saw with my own eyes
the Chosen One of righteousness and of faith,
(7a) And I saw His habitation

---

151 The same thing happened to Elijah, who also went to up to heaven without experiencing death (see II Kings 2).

152 Many will interpret verses 3-5 to be describing heaven. However, I interpret this to be part of Enoch's blessing of our generation in the here and now. I believe that he saw the reality that our homes would become places of intercession and prayer, where the angels of God would make their dwelling among us, and from which rivers of blessing would flow to flood the earth. The text says that he saw this vision while in heaven, not that he saw this vision of heaven. The amazing promise here is that ordinary families are going to begin walking the thin gold line and move from glory to glory in our generation.

under the wings of the Lord of Spirits.[153]
(6b) And righteousness will prevail in His days,
And the righteous and elect
will be without number
before Him forever and ever.[154]

(7b) And all the righteous and chosen ones before Him
will be as powerful as flaming lights,[155]
and their mouths will overflow with blessing,
And their lips will magnify
the name of the Lord of Spirits,
and righteousness will never falter in His Presence,[156]
and honor will never fail before Him.

(8) I longed to live there,
and my spirit longed for that habitation:
and so it became my portion,

---

153 See Psalm 91, describes the "secret place of the Most High." This may also be
a reference to living in continual communion with God in the Most Holy Place,
the seat of rest, which was continually overshadowed by His wings. Also, this is
where Moses would speak with God "face to face, as a man speaks with his friend"
(see Exodus 33:11, Exodus 34:30-35, Exodus 37:9, and II Corinthians 3:7-18).

154 See the "great multitude" that is beyond calculation in Revelation chapter 7.

155 Paul speaks of the "powers of the age to come," which are not yet fully
revealed. This chapter describes believers who have not only been justified (i.e.
saved) but have now been glorified, so they have spiritual abilities and qualities
that go far beyond ordinary, fallen human beings (see Hebrews 6:5, Romans 8:18,
Romans 8:29-30, and II Corinthians 3:16-18).

156 See Jude 1:24-25.

because this is what was established for me in the presence of
the Lord of Spirits.[157]

(9) In those days, I praised and proclaimed
the magnificence of the name of the Lord of Spirits
with blessings and [sweet songs],
because He destined me for blessing and glory
according to His good pleasure.

(10) For a long time, my eyes
gazed upon that place,
and I blessed Him and praised Him, saying:
'He is blessed, and may He be blessed
from the beginning and forevermore.

(11) And in Him there are no limits.
His knowledge extends [infinitely],
from before the world was created,
to what is eternal,
and to what will happen
from one generation to the next.[158]

---

157 Note that Enoch saw the redeemed who were living under New Covenant
realities and he deeply longed to be among them. In response, the Lord granted his
desire to live under a New Covenant reality. Note that faith, love, and hunger for
God unlocked this reality in his life.

158 In this verse, Enoch is filled with awe and wonder because his own experience
of being with God outside of space and time, in the eternal realms of glory, causes
him to become lost in the infinite nature of God, who is omnipresent, eternal, and
omniscient.

(12) Those who never sleep bless You:[159]
they stand before Your glory
and bless, praise, and exalt [You], saying:

"Holy, holy, holy,
is the Lord of Spirits:
He fills the earth with spirits."[160]

(13) And here my eyes saw
all those who never sleep:
they stand before Him and bless [Him], saying:

'You are Blessed,
and blessed is the name of the Lord
forever and ever.'
(14) And my face was changed
because I could not take in any more.[161]

---

159 It might be a good idea to stay up an extra hour to pray occasionally. Jesus
sometimes prayed all night, as did many on the thin gold line.

160 See Isaiah 6:3: Tthis is similar to Isaiah's wording, except that Enoch used the
word "spirits" instead of glory. One possibility is that the spirits Enoch is referring
to are angels who provide the canopy of glory that rests over the earth.

161 See Exodus 34:29: This is the point at which Enoch had beheld so much
glory that his face was already shining like Moses when he descended from Sinai
after meeting with God face to face. Enoch couldn't take any more of God's glory
and needed to take a break.

The Archangels Worship the Lord of Glory

40

(1) And after that
I saw thousands of thousands
and ten thousand times ten thousand,[162]
I saw a multitude beyond
number or calculation,
who stood before the Lord of Spirits.[163]

(2) And on the four sides of the Lord of Spirits
I saw four presences,
different from those that do not sleep,
and I learned their names:
For the angel that went with me
told me their names,
and showed me all the hidden things.

(3) And I heard the voices
of those four presences
as they showered praises
upon the Lord of glory.

(4) The first voice blesses
the Lord of Spirits
forever and ever.

---

162 100,000,000

163 See Revelation 7: Enoch is again seeing the same "great multitude" that John
saw coming out of the Great Tribulation.

(5) And the second voice I heard
blesses the Elect One
and the elect ones who
depend on the Lord of Spirits.

(6) And the third voice I heard
pray and intercede for everyone
who lives on the earth [and everyone who]
intercedes in the name of the Lord of Spirits.

(7) And I heard the fourth voice
fending off the accusers
and forbidding them
from coming before the Lord of Spirits
to accuse those who live on the earth.[164]

(8) After that I asked
the angel of peace who went with me,
who showed me everything that is hidden:

'Who are these four presences
which I have seen and whose words
I have heard and written down?'

---

164 Note that the first voice describes the act of worship, the second voice describes divine favor and blessing, the third voice describes prayer and intercession, and the fourth voice describes a proper understanding of legal procedure in spiritual warfare. These are four things that are essential to our generation fulfilling its purpose.

(9) And he said to me:

'This first is Michael,
the merciful and long-suffering.

And the second,
who is set over all the diseases
and all the wounds of the children of men,
is Raphael.

And the third,
who is set over all the powers,
is Gabriel.

And the fourth,
who is set over the repentance that leads to
hope of inheriting eternal life,
is named Phanuel.'[165]
And in those days,
I heard these four voices
of the four angels of the Lord of Spirits.

---

165 Phanuel means "the face of God."

God's Dominion Over the Cosmos

41

(1) And after that I saw all of
the mysteries of the heavens,
and how this realm is structured, and how the
actions of men
are weighed in the balance.

(2) And there I saw the mansions of the chosen ones
and the mansions of holy [people],
and I saw there with my own eyes
all the sinners who deny the name of the Lord
being driven from there, and being dragged off:
they could not stay there because of the punishment
that proceeds from the Lord of Spirits.

(3) And there my eyes saw
the mysteries of the lightning and thunder,
and the mysteries of the winds,
how they are separated
as they blow over the earth,
and the secrets of the clouds and dew,
and I saw their source there in that place
from which [they gush]
to saturate the dusty soil.

(4) And there I saw closed chambers
out of which the winds are divided,
the chamber of the hail and winds,
the chamber of the mist,

and [the chamber] of the clouds,
and the cloud that has
hovered over the earth
since the beginning of the world.[166]

(5) And I saw the chambers of the sun and moon,
which they come out from and return to,
and their glorious setting,
and how one is superior to the other,
and their stately orbit,[167]
and how they do not leave their orbit,
and they add nothing to their orbit
and they take nothing from it,
and they keep faith with each other,

in accordance with the oath
by which they are bound together.[168]

---

166 Compare the description of this last cloud to Genesis 1:2.

167 Many of Enoch's descriptions of nature challenge our belief by referring
to strange "chambers" and "portals." At the same time, he seems to be aware of
orbits and even describes the law of gravity in this passage. This strange duality of
scientific accuracy and bizarre description may reflect a deeper truth, that the seen
world is undergirded and proceeds from the heavenly realm. We understand the
laws of science based on our observation of the physical world. However, the Spirit
realm is something that we are only beginning to understand. It is a good thing to
acknowledge that we don't have all the answers.

168 The "oath that binds them together" could be interpreted as the law of gravity, a remarkable scientific observation for this ancient prophet.

(6) And first the sun goes out
and traces his path according to the
decree of the Lord of Spirits,
and mighty is His name forever and ever.

(7) And after that I saw [both] the hidden
and the visible path of the moon,
and she completes her designated path
in that place by day and by night—
each having opposite positions
before the Lord of Spirits.
And they give thanks and praise
and never rest;
for giving thanks is their rest.
(8) The sun often changes
for a blessing or a curse,[169]
and the course of the path of the moon
is light to the righteous
and darkness to those who sin
against the name of the Lord,
Who made a separation
between the light and the darkness,
and divided the spirits of men,
and strengthened the spirits of the righteous,
because of His own righteousness.

---

169 This refers to solar eclipses, which often have some spiritual significance (see Joel 2:31).

(9) For no angel can change these things
and no power is able to hinder them;
for He appoints a judge for them all
and He judges everyone before Him.

42

(1) [When] Wisdom found no place
where she could live,
then a dwelling place was
assigned to her in the heavens.[170]
(2) Wisdom went out to make her dwelling
among the children of men,
and found nowhere that she could dwell:
so Wisdom returned to her place,
and took her seat among the angels.

(3) And then Unrighteousness[171]
came out from her chambers:
She found those she did not even need to seek
and made her place with them,

---

170 Wisdom is often described as a rejected woman in Scripture (see Proverbs 1:20-33).

171 This refers to a different entity, Unrighteousness, which is the opposite of Wisdom. This verse points out the fact that those who reject wisdom will end up living with unrighteousness. You're going to end up living with one of these companions. Which would you rather have?

like rain in a desert and dew on a thirsty land.[172]

43 (1) And I saw other lightnings
and the stars of heaven,
and I saw how
He called them all by their names[173]
and they listened attentively to Him.

(2) And I saw how they are weighed
in a righteous balance according to
how much light they are given:
I saw the magnitude of space between them
and the day of their appearing,
and how their spinning produces lightning:
and I saw how the [number of them] circling
corresponds to the number of the angels,
and how they rely on each other.

(3) And I asked the angel who went with me
and who showed me hidden things:
'What are these?'

(4) And he said to me:

---

172 This imagery in the Bible usually refers to the Holy Spirit, who comes as refreshing water to spiritually dry hearts. However, in this case, this metaphor is describing how unrighteousness will completely saturate our lives if we open the door to it. People often give in to unrighteousness to fill the needs and desires that the Holy Spirit is meant to satisfy.

173 See Isaiah 40:26.

'The Lord of Spirits
has showed you what they symbolize:
these are the names of the holy
who dwell on the earth
and believe in the name
of the Lord of Spirits
forever and ever.'[174]

44

(1) Also I saw another wonder regarding the lightnings: when some of the stars rise, they will become lightnings and won't be able to leave their new form.[175]

---

174 Note that God told Abraham that the stars also represent his seed, or the number of his children. This refers to all of those who, like him, encounter God and are justified by faith (see Genesis 15:5, Genesis 22:17, and Romans 4:9). This chapter suggests that there is great heavenly glory for all who God has called into His kingdom.

175 Here we see the concept of the glorified believer. Note the context here: The previous verses compared stars with redeemed mankind. A more provocative interpretation of this verse is that some of the saints will "become lightnings" and remain clothed in a high level of power and glory forever, unable to return to the corrupted bodies and boring lives that preceded their glorification. For a biblical parallel, note that in I Corinthians 15:35-58, Paul describes the vast difference between our "earthly bodies" and our "heavenly bodies" and in I John 3:2, John the Beloved marvels at the fact that, "what we will be has not yet been made known." There is glory that goes beyond description in store for all who live in Him.

The Second Prophecy

CHAPTERS 45-57

When Christ Judges Men and Angels

45 (1) This is the second prophecy,
concerning those who deny the name
of the dwelling of the holy ones
and the Lord of Spirits.

(2) They will not ascend to heaven,
and they will not be on the earth.
This will be the destiny of the sinners
who have denied the name of the Lord of Spirits:
they will remain until
the day of suffering and tribulation.

(3) On that day my Chosen One
will sit on the throne of glory[176]
and will judge what they have done,
and their graves will be countless,
and their souls will grow [jealous]
when they see My chosen ones,
And those who have called upon
My glorious name:

(4) Then I will cause My Chosen One
to dwell with them.[177]

---

176 This speaks of the Messiah. See Matthew 25:31 for a similar description from the Messiah Himself.

177 See Revelation 21:3.

And I will transform the heaven[178]
and make it an eternal blessing and light.[179]
(5) And I will transform the earth
and make it a blessing,
and I will let My chosen ones live there:
but the sinners and evildoers
will not set foot on it.

(6) For My righteous ones are satisfied
by the peace that I have given to them[180]
[because I] have caused them to live in my Presence:[181]
But for the sinners there is judgment brewing in Me,
so I will remove them from the face of the earth.

46

(1) And there I saw One
who had a Head of Days,[182]
and His head was white like wool,
and with Him was another being
whose countenance
had the appearance of a man,

---

178 See Revelation 21:1.

179 See Isaiah 30:26.

180 See John 14:27.

181 If you want to have the peace of Christ, then make every effort to live in His Presence continually.

182 Compare this chapter with John's vision of the glorified Christ in Revelation 1:12-20 and Daniel 7:9-10. There are too many similarities between Enoch's writings and these texts to fully document in the footnotes.

and His face was full of grace,
like one of the holy angels.

(2) And I asked the angel who went with me
and showed me all the hidden things,
concerning that Son of Man,[183]
who was He, and where did He come from,
and why did he have a Head of Days?[184]

[3] And he answered and said:
This is the Son of Man who has righteousness,
and righteousness dwells with Him,
and He reveals all the treasures
that have been hidden,
because the Lord of Spirits has chosen Him,
and His place is to have supremacy
before the Lord of Spirits
in perfection forever.[185]

(4) And this Son of Man whom you have seen
will raise up the kings
and the mighty from their seats,

---

183 Jesus often referred to Himself using this title to show that He had taken on all the natural characteristics of humanity.

184 This phrase is similar to the "Ancient of Days" title of Daniel 7. However, the phrase "Head of Days" provides another layer of meaning, because it points to the fact that Christ is the firstborn of Creation and has Lordship over the realms of time and space.

185 See Colossians 1:15-19.

and the strong from their thrones[186]
and will loosen the reins of the strong,
and break the teeth of the sinners.[187]

(5) And He will cast down the kings[188]
from their thrones and kingdoms
who do not exalt and praise Him,
or humbly acknowledge the source from
which their authority was given.

(6) And He will cast down
the reputation of the strong,
and will fill them with shame.
And they will live in darkness,
with worms as their bed,
and they will have no hope

---

186 This probably speaks of raising up the righteous "kings of the earth," who
will rise from their places of rest, walk in His light, go into battle with Him, and
rule and reign with Him (see Revelation 21:24). This is a different group than the
unrighteous kings of the earth who wage war against Him, which are discussed
in the rest of this chapter (see Revelation 19:19). There are two groups of kings
because one represents the unrighteous government and spiritual powers that have
ruled this world in darkness, and the second represents eternal and righteous rul-
ership under the supremacy of Christ. This is why when He rides into battle with
the armies of heaven, the names that are written on His thigh are "King of kings"
and "Lord of lords" (see Revelation 19:16). These names are written on His thigh,
because they are the kings that He Himself has sired by His Spirit, the very sons of
God who have now been given authority and power to rule and reign with Him.

187 See Psalm 3:7.

188 This chapter is best read alongside Psalm 2.

of rising from their beds,
because they do not exalt
the name of the Lord of Spirits.

(7) And these are those
who [mis]judge the stars of heaven,
and raise their hands against the Most High,
and tread upon the earth and live in it.
and all their deeds are wicked,
and their power rests upon their riches,
and their faith is in the gods
that they have made with their hands,
and they deny the name of the Lord of Spirits.

(8) And they persecute
the houses of His congregations,[189]
and the faithful who depend upon
the name of the Lord of Spirits.

47 (1) And in those days,
the cry of the righteous will rise,
and the blood of the righteous
will ascend from the earth
and it will reach the Lord of Spirits.[190]

---

189 This phrase probably describes churches and synagogues.

190 See Revelation 6:9.

(2) In those days, the holy ones
who live in the heavens above
will unite with one voice
and petition, pray, praise, give thanks,
and bless the name of the Lord of Spirits
on behalf of the blood of the righteous
which has been shed.
And the prayer of the righteous
will not be without significance
in the Presence of the Lord of Spirits,
so that judgment may be executed on their behalf,
and so that they will not have to suffer forever.

(3) In those days, I saw the Head of Days
when He seated Himself
upon the throne of His glory,
and the books of the living
were opened before Him:[191]
and all His host which is in heaven above
and His counselors stood before Him,

(4) And the hearts of the holy overflowed with joy;
because the number of the righteous was now offered,
and the cry of the righteous was now heard,
and the blood of the righteous was now summoned
before the Lord of Spirits.

---

191 See Daniel 7:9-10.

Enoch's Revelation of Jesus Christ

48

(1) And in that place I saw
the fountain of righteousness
which was inexhaustible:
and around it were many fountains of wisdom;
and everyone who was thirsty drank from them,
and they were filled with wisdom,
and they lived with the righteous and holy and elect.

(2) At that hour, the Son of Man was named
in the Presence of the Lord of Spirits,
and His name [was announced] before the first day.[192]

(3) Yes, before the sun and the signs were created,
before the stars of the heaven were made,
His name was named before the Lord of Spirits.[193]
(4) He shall be a staff to the righteous
they will lean on Him
to brace themselves and not fall,[194]
and He will be the light of the Gentiles,[195]

---

192 This speaks of Jesus Christ, who was "the lamb slain before the foundations of the world" (see Revelation 13:8).

193 See John 1.

194 See Jude 1:24-25 for a beautiful exposition of this truth. We can lean on the Lord when we are weak, just as an old man leans on a staff when he needs support.

195 See Isaiah 42:6-7, Isaiah 49:6.

and the Hope of those whose hearts are troubled.[196]

(5) All who live on the earth
will fall down and worship Him,
and will praise and bless
and celebrate the Lord of Spirits with song.
(6) And this was the purpose He was chosen for,
and it was hidden in Him
before the creation of the world and eternally.

(7) And the wisdom of the Lord of Spirits
has revealed Him to the holy and righteous;
because He has protected
the inheritance of the righteous,
for they have hated and despised
this world of unrighteousness,
and have hated all of its works and ways
in the name of the Lord of Spirits:
for in His name they are saved,[197]
and their lives are lived in His great pleasure.

(8) In these days, the kings of the earth
will become completely depressed,
along with the strong who possess the land
through what they have made;

---

196 Jesus may have referenced this directly (see John 14:1,27).

197 See Acts 4:12.

for on the day of their anguish and affliction
they will not be able to save themselves.

(9) And I will hand them over
to the hands of My chosen ones:[198]
just as straw burns up in the fire,[199]
so will they be consumed before
the face of the holy:
they will sink before the face of the righteous
just like lead sinks in the water
and no trace of them will be found again.

(10) And on the day of their affliction
the earth will rest, and before them
they will fall and never rise again:
And there will be no one
who can take them in his hands
and resurrect them again:
for they have denied
the Lord of Spirits and His anointed.
May the name of the Lord of Spirits be blessed.

---

198 When read in full, this verse suggests that the evil rulers of this world will
be judged by redeemed and glorified believers, whose faces will radiate with such
holiness and righteousness that no one will even be able to stand before them. I
Corinthians 6:2-3 makes it clear that believers will judge both humans and angels
in the age to come.

199 See Isaiah 5:24, Isaiah 29:5.

The Ever-Increasing Glory of God

49 (1) For wisdom is poured out like water,
and the glory that proceeds from Him
will forever [expand and increase].

(2) For His power is made known
through all of the mysteries of righteousness,
and unrighteousness
will disappear like a shadow,
and will no longer be there;
because the Chosen One
stands before the Lord of Spirits,
and His glory is ever-increasing,
and His power is revealed to all generations.

(3) And in Him dwells the spirit of wisdom,
and the spirit of counsel,
And the spirit of understanding and of power,[200]

And the spirits of those
who have fallen asleep in righteousness.

(4) And He will judge the secret things,
and no one will be able to speak
even one untrue word before him;[201]

---

200 See Isaiah 11:2-5 for a parallel to this verse.

201 See Luke 12:3.

for He is the Chosen One
before the Lord of Spirits
according to His good pleasure.

The Glorification of the Saints

50 (1) And in those days a transformation
will happen to the holy and elect,
And the light of the sun
will remain on them,[202]
And glory and honor
will be transferred to the holy,
(2) on the day of affliction
on which evil is already stored up
against the sinners.
And the righteous will be victorious
in the name of the Lord of Spirits:
and He will cause the others to see this
so that they may repent[203]
and abandon their idols.

---

202 See Matthew 13:43, Isaiah 30:26.

203 This is a strange verse. On one hand, it appears to be discussing the transformation of the redeemed when they receive their glorified bodies. However, this verse implies that this transformation will begin in the time before Christ comes, so that sinners may see this glory rise upon them and turn to the Lord. Isaiah 60:1-3 may help to unravel this mystery: Some apply this promise only to the second coming Christ, but many believe this is a promise for the last generation, who will bring in the great harvest of souls.

(3) They will have no honor
through the name of the Lord of Spirits,
but through His name they will be saved,[204]
and the Lord of Spirits
will have compassion on them,
for His compassion is enormous.
(4) And He is also right in all of His judgment,[205]
and in the presence of His glory
unrighteousness will not be able to save itself:[206]
at His judgment, the unrepentant
will crumble before Him.[207]

(5) And from this point on,
I will have no mercy on them,
says the Lord of Spirits.

---

204 Paul addresses the difference between salvation and reward in depth in
II Corinthians 3:10-15. Many believers will be saved, but will have no further
reward because, after trusting in Christ for salvation, they invested all of their time
and resources in carnal pursuits instead of investing their lives in what the Spirit
desires.

205 Note that before the judgment seat of Christ, there is both great compassion
and great righteousness because He is the embodiment of both. No one will be
able to accuse Him of being either unmerciful or unjust.

206 This confirms that nothing will be hidden from the eyes of the Lord on the
Day of Judgment.

207 Several verses in this chapter imply that there is one final chance to repent.
This seems counter to evangelical teaching, but may be related to the mystery
of the "multitudes" that are in the "valley of decision" in Joel 3:14. However,
when taken in whole, this chapter calls us to judge our own lives with fear and
trembling, and not develop spiritual complacency or misuse the grace of God to
tolerate sin in our lives.

The Restoration of All Things

51 (1) And in those days the earth will give up
that which has been entrusted to it,
and Sheol will also give back
those it has received,
and hell will give back that which it owes.
for in those days the Chosen One will ascend,
(2) and He will select the righteous
and holy from among them:
for the day has now come for them to be saved.[208]

(3) And in those days,
the Chosen One will sit on My throne,[209]
and His mouth will declare
all the secrets of wisdom and counsel:
For the Lord of Spirits has given them to Him
and has glorified Him.[210]

---

208 This most likely refers to the resurrections that took place when Jesus died on the cross. These were those who were redeemed by looking forward to His redemption and received the fruit of redemption when He was crucified. This verse seems to be describing Jesus hand-selecting which ones in Sheol should be raised at this time. See Matthew 27:51-53 for more clarity on this strange event.

209 Note that Jesus ascended to the right hand of God, where He is enthroned forever (see Mark 16:19, Luke 22:69, and Acts 2:33).

210 See Isaiah 11:2, Revelation 4:5, and Revelation 5:6. Note that the seven spirits of God are before the throne and that these are the eyes of the Lamb.

(4) And in those days
the mountains will leap like rams,
and the hills will skip
like lambs satisfied with milk,[211]
And the faces of all the angels in heaven
will be lit up with joy.

(5b) And the earth will rejoice,
(c) and the righteous will live on it,
(d) And the chosen will walk on it.

Mountains Melt Before the Lord

52 (1) And after those days,
in that place where I had seen
all of these visions of what is hidden—

I was carried off in a whirlwind
and they carried me towards the west—

(2) There I saw with my own eyes
all the secret things of heaven that will be:
a mountain of iron,
and a mountain of copper,
and a mountain of silver,
and a mountain of gold,

---

211 See Psalm 114:4.

and a mountain of soft metal,
and a mountain of lead.

(3) And I asked the angel who went with me:
'What things are these which I have seen in secret?'

(4) And he said to me:
'All these things which you have seen
will be under the dominion of His Anointed
that He may be powerful and mighty on the earth.'

(5) And then the angel of peace explained:
'Wait a little, and all of the secret things
which surround the Lord of Spirits
will be revealed to you.[212]

(6) And these mountains
which your eyes have seen,
the mountain of iron,
and the mountain of copper,
and the mountain of silver,
and the mountain of gold,
and the mountain of soft metal,
and the mountain of lead:

---

212 Notice that Enoch had to "wait a little" to receive more revelation from
God. Lingering in God's Presence is often a key to receiving higher and deeper
revelation.

all of these will melt like wax before the fire[213]
in the presence of the Chosen One
and like the water which streams down
from the tops of these mountains,
and they will become powerless at His feet.[214]
(7) And it will happen in those days
that none will be saved,
by gold or by silver,[215]
And none will be able to escape.

(8) And there will be no iron for war,
nor will one clothe himself with a breastplate.
Bronze will be useless,

---

213 Many will interpret this chapter to be simply metaphorical; however, the possibility remains that this could be describing realms of heaven that are completely foreign to us and outside of our limited frame of reference. Regardless, consider the amount of energy that it would take to reduce seven mountains that are made entirely of metal to mere puddles in a moment. This only begins to describe the power that is in Christ and the fiery glory that proceeds from the Ancient of Days like a river (see Daniel 7). There is a strange mystery here worthy of exploration, because even Peter said that "the elements will melt in the heat" on the day of the Lord (see II Peter 3:12).

214 Enoch has listed the mountains (iron, copper, silver, gold, soft metal, and lead) in the precise order of their metal's nuclear binding energies, something that would have been unlikely without Divine inspiration. Binding energy determines an element's classification in the Periodic Table, with iron (and one isotope, nickel-62) being the most tightly bound. Elements to the right of iron (heavier) are capable of fission, while elements to the left (lighter) are capable of fusion. The soft metal is likely thallium, soft enough to be cut with a butter knife, and classified between gold and lead.

215 See I Peter 1:7, 1:18.

and tin will be of no service and will not be valued,
and lead will not be desired.

(9) And all these things will be
[denied and] destroyed from the surface of the earth,
when the Chosen One appears
before the face of the Lord of Spirits.'[216]

Judgement, Banishment, and War

53 (1) There, I saw with my own eyes
a deep valley with open gates,
and all who live on the earth
and the islands [of the] sea
will bring gifts to it
and offerings and tribute,
but that deep valley will never become full.

(2) Their hands commit anarchic deeds,
and the sinners devour all those
that they oppress without just cause:
but these sinners will be destroyed
before the face of the Lord of Spirits,
and they will be removed from the face of His earth,
and they will perish once and for all.

---

216 These metals could be rejected under the millennial reign of Christ because
God will give us materials that are more valuable than these.

(3) For I saw all the angels of punishment
abiding there and sharpening
all of the instruments of Satan.

(4) And I asked the angel of peace who was with me:
'For whom are they sharpening these instruments?'

(5) And he said to me:
'They sharpen these for the kings
and the mighty [rulers] of this earth,
and they will be destroyed by them.[217]

(6) And after this,
the Righteous and Chosen One
will cause the house of His congregation to appear:[218]
from then on they will no longer be hindered
in the name of the Lord of Spirits.

(7) And these mountains will not remain
[on] the earth in the Presence of His righteousness,
but the hills will gush like a fountain of water,[219]
and the righteous will have rest
from the oppression of sinners.'

---

217 See Revelation 19:17-18.

218 This probably refers to the New Jerusalem descending (see Revelation 21).

219 This could also refer to Jerusalem, which is a city with many hills and hidden aquifers.

54

(1) And I looked and turned
to another part of the earth,
and saw there a deep valley
with burning fire.

(2) And they brought the kings
and the powerful, and began
to cast them into this deep valley.
(3) And I saw with my own eyes
how they made their instruments,
iron chains of immeasurable weight.[220]

(4) And I asked the angel of peace who was with me:
'Who are these chains for?'

(5) And he said to me:
'These are being prepared
for the hosts of Azazel,
so that they can take them and cast them
into the abyss of complete condemnation,
and they will cover their jaws with rough stones
as the Lord of Spirits has commanded.

(6) And Michael, Gabriel, Raphael, and Phanuel
will take hold of them on that great day,
and cast them on that day into the burning furnace,
so that the Lord of Spirits

---

220 See Psalm 2:3, II Peter 2:4, and Jude 1:6.

will bring vengeance on them
for their unrighteousness
because they became servants to Satan
and led astray those who live on the earth.'

[Verses 7-9 of Chapter 54 and verses 1-2 of Chapter 55 are not included in *Enoch's Blessing* because these are noted by the scribes as fragments of the Book of Noah and belong with another book, which was scribed into the same scroll. The removed section described the great flood, not the final judgment. See the introduction for a fuller explanation.]

55

(3) I have chosen to detain them
by the hand of the angels
on the day of tribulation and pain
because of this.

I will allow My penalty
and My wrath to rest on them
says God, the Lord of Spirits.

(4) You mighty kings who live on the earth,
you will be forced to behold My Chosen One,
how He sits on the throne of glory
and judges Azazel,
and all of [his] underlings,
and all of his armies
in the name of the Lord of Spirits.'

56

(1) And I saw there the armies of
the angels of punishment marching,
and they held scourges[221]
and chains of iron and bronze.
(2) And I asked the angel of peace who was with me:
'Where are these who hold the scourges going to?'

(3) And he said to me:
'To their chosen and cherished ones,[222]
to cast them into the chasm of the abyss of the valley.

(4) And then that valley will be filled
with their chosen and cherished ones,
and the days of their lives will end,
and from this point on,
the days of their deception will be over.

(5) And in those days, the angels will return
and hurl themselves to the east
upon the Persians and Medes:[223]
they will stir up the kings,
so that a spirit of unrest will come upon them,
and they will rouse them from their thrones,

---

221 or whips

222 This refers to the "chosen and cherished ones" of the fallen angels.

223 This could be a prophecy pertaining to the conflict between Israel, Iran, and other nations in the Middle East.

that they will come out like lions from their lairs,
and like hungry wolves among the flocks.

(6) And they will go up and march
on the land of His chosen ones,[224]
and the land of His chosen ones
will be a threshing-floor
and a highway in front of them.

(7) But the city of my righteous
will be a hindrance to their horses.
and they will begin to fight among themselves,
and their power will turn against themselves,
and a man will not recognize his brother,
nor a son his father or his mother,
until the number of corpses there
is beyond calculation because of the slaughter,
and their punishment is not in vain.

(8) In those days Sheol will open its jaws,
and they will be swallowed up by it
and their destruction will be complete;
Sheol will devour the sinners
in the presence of the elect.'

---

224 This most likely refers to Israel and the final conflict of Revelation chapter 20.

57

(1) And after this, I saw this happen:
I saw another army of wagons,
and men riding on them,
and coming on the winds from the east,
and from the west to the south.[225]

(2) And the noise of their wagons was heard,
and when this turmoil took place
the holy ones from heaven noticed it,
and the pillars of the earth
were moved from their place,
and the sound of it was heard[226]
from one end of heaven to the other,
in one day.

(3) And they will all fall down
and worship the Lord of Spirits.
This is the end of the second prophecy.

---

225 This is an intriguing verse: These "armies in wagons" and those who are "coming on the winds" could refer to the modern machinery of war, such as tanks and planes.

226 Some might interpret the previous three lines to be describing an atomic bomb, which also "moves the pillars of the earth" and carries a sonic blast.

The Third Prophecy

CHAPTERS 58-59

Living in the Light of the Lord

58

(1) And I began to declare the third prophecy concerning the righteous and chosen:[227]
(2) You are blessed,
you righteous and elect,
because your inheritance is glorious.

(3) The righteous will live
in the light of the sun,[228]
and the chosen in
the light of eternal life:
the days of their life will never end,
and the days of these holy people
will be beyond comprehension.[229]

(4) And they will search for light
and find righteousness in the Lord of Spirits:[230]
there will be peace upon the righteous
in the name of the Eternal Lord.

(5) And after this, it will be said
to the holy in heaven
that they should seek out

---

227 This chapter contains yet another list of blessings for the last generation of this age.

228 See Malachi 4:2 and Matthew 13:43.

229 See I Corinthians 2:9.

230 See Romans 3:22.

the secrets of righteousness,
the heritage of faith:
for it has become as bright as the sun
upon the earth,
and the darkness is past.

(6) And there will be a light that never ends,
and they will never come to an end of days,
for the darkness will be destroyed first,
And the light established
in the Presence of the Lord of Spirits
and the light of honor
will be established forever
before the Lord of Spirits.

The Secrets of the Lightnings

59 (1) In those days, my eyes saw
the secrets of the lightnings,
and of the lights,
and the judgments that they execute:
and they strike for a blessing
or a curse as the Lord of Spirits wills.

(2) And there I saw
the secrets of the thunder,
and how when it resounds above in the heaven,
the sound of it is heard,
and He allowed me to see the judgments

being released on the earth,
whether they were for well-being and blessing,
or for a curse according to the Word
of the Lord of Spirits.[231]

(3) And after that all the secrets
of the lights and lightnings
were shown to me:
they strike for blessing and are fulfilled.[232]

---

231 In Scripture, thunder and lightning are often connected to the release of
the Word of the Lord and the great power that proceeds from God's Presence
(see Psalm 29:7 and Psalm 18:12). Lightning is also related to the moving of the
Seraphim, as in Ezekiel chapter 1.

232 The release of lightning on the earth also signifies the release of accumulated
intercession in heaven (see Revelation 8:1-2). Some have also suggested that it
describes glorified believers who move in the power and authority of Jesus Christ.

Topical Index

Abel, 22:7

Abyss, 10:13, 18:11-12, 21:7

Accusation
fending off accusers, 40:7

Angels
cherubim, 14:11, 14:18
fallen, see fallen angels
forms they take, 17:1
imparting revelation, 1:2
in great numbers, 14:22, 40:1
in righteous homes, 39:4-5
never sleep, 39:13
punishers, 53:3, 56:1
paths they take, 18:5

Archangels
Gabriel, 9:1, 20:7, 40:9, 54:6
Michael, 9:1, 20:5, 40:9, 54:6
Phanuel, 40:9, 54:6
Raguel, 20:4, 23:4
Raphael, 9:1, 20:3, 22:3, 40:9, 54:6
Remiel, 20:8
Saraqael, 20:6
Uriel, 9:1, 19:1, 20:2, 21:5, 21:9, 27:2

Astrology
taught by fallen angels, 8:2

Blessings
for final generation, 1:8, 5:7-9, 58:1-6
for the earth, 28
for the righteous, 85
storehouses of, 11:1

Blood
defilement of, 7:5
destruction of mixed bloodlines, 10:9, 22:7
innocent blood crying out, 47:1
of the righteous, 47:1, 47:4
preservation of pure bloodline, 10:3

Canopy
God coming out of His, 1:3
of heaven, 18:5
over paradise, 20:7

Chosen ones, 1:1, 5:7a
jealousy of, 45:3
land of, 56:6
light shining from, 38:2
role in the final judgment, 48:9

Christ
Ancient of Days (Head of Days), 46:1-2
chosen before foundation of world, 48:2, 48:6
dominion of, 22:14, 52:4
Eternal King, 25:5-7
garments whiter than snow, 14:20

scientific classification, 3:1
(see notes for chapter 52)
transformation at end of age, 45:4-5

Crystal
former crystal house, 14:9-14
latter crystal house, 14:15-19
(aka New Jerusalem)

Desire
to be among the righteous, 39:8

Earth
as an inheritance, 5:7b
crying out, 7:6, 9:2
fountains of the deep, 17:7-8
filled with God's goodness, 25:3
restoration of, 10:18-20
rejoicing of, 51:5b

Enoch
as a scribe, 12:4, 15:1
call from God, 14:24
face changed, 39:14
hidden, 12:1
his ability to see prophetically, 37:4
lifted by whirlwind, 14:8, 39:3, 52:1
preaching to all generations, 37:2-3, 37:5

Eternal life
as a free gift, 37:4
comes through the righteousness of the Lord, 58:3-4

Made in United States
North Haven, CT
28 April 2024

51829113R00104